From Neighborhood to Nation

Civil Society: Historical and Contemporary Perspectives

BRIAN O'CONNELL
Civil Society: The Underpinnings of American Democracy

PHILLIP H. ROUND
By Nature and by Custom Cursed: Transatlantic Civil Discourse and New England Cultural Production, 1620–1660

BOB EDWARDS, MICHAEL W. FOLEY, AND MARIO DIANI, EDS.
Beyond Tocqueville: Civil Society and the Social Capital Debate in Comparative Perspective

KEN THOMSON
From Neighborhood to Nation: The Democratic Foundations of Civil Society

From Neighborhood to Nation

The Democratic Foundations of Civil Society

Ken Thomson

Tufts University
Published by University Press of New England
Hanover and London

Tufts University
Published by University Press of New England, Hanover, NH 03755
© 2001 by Ken Thomson
All rights reserved
Printed in the United States of America
5 4 3 2 1

Library of Congress Cataloging-in-Publication Data

Thomson, Ken, 1946–
    From neighborhood to nation : the democratic foundations of civil
society / Ken Thomson.
        p. cm.—(Civil society)
Includes bibliographical references (p.) and index.
    ISBN 1–58465–104–0 (cloth : alk. paper)—ISBN 1–58465–105–9 (pbk. :
alk. paper)
    1. Citizens' associations—United States. 2. Neighborhood
government—United States. 3. Municipal government—United States.
4. Democracy—United States. 5. Political participation—United States.
I. Title. II. Series.
JS303.5 .T56 2001
306.2'0973—dc21   2001002135

Contents

Tables

Preface

I was walking back to the subway with a friend after an inspiring memorial service for George Sommaripa, a visionary of the peace movement in our nation. For more than thirty years, George had been the one who always seemed a step ahead of the rest of us in planning the next strategy for action. My friend and I fell into a discussion of the book I was working on, *From Neighborhood to Nation*. As I described how its principles were based upon the framework of face-to-face meetings not unlike those that he and I had been to thousands of times with leaders like George, my friend threw up his hands in dismay. "I'm frustrated and discouraged with our government. It seems totally out of control, in the hands of special interests out to line their own pockets. But I don't see how this would work. There has to be some way to translate the discussions of citizens into national policy. It would take a complete change of our government, amendments to the constitution, the whole ball of wax. I don't see how this is realistic at all." At that point, our trains arrived and we had to go our separate ways, for that day.

As Americans, this is our problem and our potential. Democracy is our heritage. Yet we know that we have serious failings and structural faults with our democracy today. Historically, we are in new territory, with a "wired" electorate with more material goods and greater skills and information to deal with complex governmental issues than ever before. We also have a public that is distracted from political life and distanced by the limits of the electronic media that have often overtaken the face-to-face politics that used to be the norm.

Too often, we throw up our hands at the entrenched interests, the maddeningly unresponsive bureaucracy, the slow prospect of democratic change. Improving our democracy, let alone changing its shape to approach anything like participatory democracy, looks like an impossible task. It's at times like these that I think back on George's wisdom. He kept asking the tough questions, and he urged us to keep our eyes on the road toward the shared future that we collectively envisioned. He articulated the obvious truths and advocated returning to the hard, basic facts. He wanted us to be realistic about what we thought would really work for the country, not what we thought would be politically saleable at the moment. He sometimes called for what seemed impractical, but it often turned out to be the most reasonable alternative in the long run— as when he advocated moving troops back from the borders between NATO and Warsaw Pact countries in Europe, at the time a stance totally opposed to conventional military wisdom and the "practical" advice of many in the peace movement. Two years later, when the Berlin wall and soon thereafter the Soviet Union fell, this withdrawal and much more became an accomplished fact.

The lessons that George applied again and again in the peace movement, we can apply in the effort for strong democracy. If we know that flaws in our democratic system will lead to increasing inequities and gridlock, to increasing alienation and tearing of the body public, we need to take stock of where we are and where we are going. We need to get back to the facts of how our communities work and understand what strengths and untapped resources we can build upon to meet these threats.

From Neighborhood to Nation reviews some of the most fundamental features of our democracy, how it prospers in our communities, and how it can grow to better meet the needs of our people in the twenty-first century. This book branches out from the work of the National Citizen Participation Development Project (NCPDP) at Tufts University's Lincoln Filene Center, and the major book produced by the Project, *The Rebirth of Urban Democracy*. The earlier work encompassed an enormous range of material dealing with the impact of citizen participation on five cities, based on extensive interviews, issues analysis, and survey polling of participants and nonparticipants, as well as respondents from ten matched cities nationwide. But it left largely untouched the rich local material we were able to glean from the hours of discussions with neighborhood leaders and survey samples stratified by neighborhood—material that would enable comparison of neighborhoods and participation in them based on specific neighborhood organizational activities. That material forms the basis of *From Neighborhood to Nation* and allows us to examine the dynamics of participation core groups and how citizens can and do build their communities, resolve differing perspectives, and learn from their successes and failures. The impact of these groups, and the potential application of our study, covers every imaginable civic issue, from the environment, housing, and land use, to crime prevention, transportation, and education.

The earlier work also hinted at the ways these forms of strong democracy in individual cities might become the core of a broader participatory democracy. *From Neighborhood to Nation* examines these possibilities in depth, looking at specific networks and deliberative structures that currently exist to bring together the efforts of such organizations and exploring the possibilities of much more extensive networks in the future. How such networks coexist with city councils, state legislatures, and Congress, now and in the coming decades, is an important part of this analysis. Participatory democracy is not only possible, its building blocks already exist, and they have provided citizens with productive roles in policymaking and in recreating their communities and, potentially, our nation.

I would like to thank Kent Portney and Jeff Berry, my best critics, colleagues, and advisors at Tufts University; they saw the importance of this work and devoted a substantial portion of their professional lives during the research phase of the NCPDP to gather some of the data from which this book grew. Without Kent, this book would never have gone beyond the Ph.D. dissertation with which it began, or included its extensive basis of public opinion survey results; without Jeff, these ideas would never have achieved their solid grounding in the democratic theory and interest group analysis that are so crucial to its key understandings. I would also like to thank Jim Ennis at Tufts for his special insights into social movement organizations, and Leonard and Susann Thomas Buckle at Northeastern University for their wisdom on the practical aspects of policy formation; along with Jeff and Kent, they composed my original dissertation committee. And a special thanks to Albert Matheny at the University of Florida for his many insightful comments on the final drafts of these chapters.

Support for the NCPDP established the framework that allowed the rich sources of data used in this book to be collected. Many thanks go to David Arnold and Michael Lipsky of the Ford Foundation, major funding providers for the NCPDP; they helped guide it through to completion. The Lincoln Filene Center at Tufts University was the home for the project. I owe a great debt to Stuart Langton, who shaped the citizen participation programs at the Center and provided oversight for the project from its beginning, and to Robert Hollister, who shepherded it through its final stages and encouraged the development of the materials that eventually became this book.

I am also grateful to all of the people, too numerous to list here, who provided support for the NCPDP. But I want to single out Frank Duehay, who provided inspiration throughout the course of this effort, Elizabeth Hall, who coordinated much of the original contacts with city and neighborhood leaders in the four cities at the core of this book, and Dorothy Shurmaster, who provided invaluable administrative assistance during the course of my work at Tufts.

I have great appreciation for the wonderful support of the University Press of New England; many thanks to Phil Pochoda and Ellen Wicklum for oversight of the publication from the beginning, to Ann Klefstad for excellent copy editing, to the production staff, especially Carol Sheehan and Ann Brash, and to Nanine Huchinson for her marketing expertise.

Ultimately, the greatest credit goes to the neighborhood leaders, city officials, and active participants of Birmingham, Dayton, Portland, and St. Paul, who made their cities into models of effective participatory democracy. People like Fay Dixon, Benjamin Greene, William Bell, Betty Bock, Charles Price, David Smalley, and Edward Speights in Birmingham; Cilla Bosnak, Bill Littlejohn, Barbara Meadows, Mike Brigner, Ollie Norris, and Sharon Alexiades in Dayton; Sarah Newhall, Rachel Jackey, Dianne Linn, Steve Rudman, Nancy Biasi, Moshe Lenske, Margaret Strachan, and Dick Crabtree in Portland; Jerry Jenkins, Lawrence Soderholm, George Latimer, Ann Copeland, Kathie Tarnowski, Roberta Megard, James Scheibel, and Paul Mandell in St. Paul; and literally hundreds of others whom we interviewed in these cities.

And finally, I'd like to thank George Sommaripa, whose vision inspired us all and continues to inspire us to keep going with the issues we know make sense, in spite of the obstacles, obsolete paradigms, and entrenched institutions that might otherwise prevent us from building better communities and a stronger democracy in the future.

Ken Thomson
April 2001

From Neighborhood to Nation

Chapter 1

Representative vs. Participatory Government

There is something different about American politics today. It is not just the sense of lost purpose in both major political parties. It is not just the strategy of derision toward government as a staple of political campaigning, or the challenges to basic election processes. It is not just the level of partisan bitterness unseen before in the lifetimes of most politicians. These discords are but multiple reflections of a trend that has been developing since at least the early 1960s: the alienation of American citizens from their government.

The persistence of this trend is perhaps best documented by Stephen Craig in *The Malevolent Leaders: Popular Discontent in America*.[1] He describes the dramatic changes in public opinion from 1964 to 1992 on such questions as "trust in political leaders to do what is right" (shifting from 22 percent to 70 percent of respondents in the lowest out of three levels of trust) and a sense of whether the country is run by "a few big interests" (shifting from 28 percent to 75 percent in the affirmative over this time period). And the return to relative social political tranquility from the turbulent 1960s did not provide a return to high trust levels, as many had predicted. Even the partial recovery of the early Reagan years proved to be short-lived, as the moderate improvement toward the end of the 1990s seems destined to be.

As Craig argues, these changes are far from superficial. They represent a fundamental dynamic in American democracy. Our institutions have undergone and continue to undergo sweeping changes. In just the last few decades we have seen party structures give way to individual candidate war chests as the driving force of political campaigns; we have seen the medium of television profoundly affect the way average Americans view national and foreign policy issues; and we have seen the number and scope of national "public interest" organizations mushroom beyond any previous expectations.

Yet the changing nature of our democracy is often unappreciated. Much of the existing political analysis of American democracy assumes that the currently predominant forms of representation and citizen participation in government are the only ones that are ever likely to exist.[2] In the same way that generals are often said to be prepared only to fight the last war, our politicians are too often prepared only to use the democratic tools of the previous era.

In the last few years, this benign neglect has begun to reverse. Widespread discussion has blossomed among both academics and practitioners about the need to bolster our "civil society." Stimulated by the widely read works of Robert Bellah[3] and Robert Putnam,[4] civil society advocates have called for a strengthening of all elements of this sector, from the family and churches to neighborhood groups and voluntary associations of all types. Their argument is that strengthening this sector will automatically strengthen trust, public-mindedness, and support for democratic values. The sector is seen to be the source of the "social capital" necessary for democracy to work. Yet, as several critics have pointed out, there is not a clear link between bowling with a local team, to use Putnam's famous example,[5] and grappling with the issues of democracy that determine how local, state, and national governments address policy issues.[6] In addition, the evidence for a decline in voluntary association involvement is not nearly as strong as Putnam suggests, according to other major studies.[7] Participation in some traditional organizations may be declining, but it is often replaced by participation in new types of organizations, including citizen advocacy groups and even, more and more often, electronic networks.

A central question in the civil society debate, therefore, is what forms of organizations and activities have the potential to bridge the yawning gap between citizens and their governments? The internal dynamics of such organizations, and in particular the nature of "public deliberation" that takes place in them, is seen by careful observers as essential. As Jean Cohen notes in her critique of civil society:

The deliberative genesis and justification of public policies or decisions deeply affecting the public in political and civil public spaces respectively must be seen as *constitutive* of the modern form of democracy. This means that wherever important decisions, or developments are occurring—be it in the scientific, corporate, media, or educational establishments—public spaces involving criticism, articulation of alternatives, and counterpowers must be provided for and protected. This, in my view, is the *sine qua non* for trust and confidence in institutions to be maintainable and warranted.[8]

These characteristics of deliberation, and the organizational forms necessary to implement them, are what I will refer to in this book as "participatory democracy." The use of this term does not imply an elimination of our current forms, which might be summed up as "representative democracy." Nor is it intended to imply involvement of all the people all the time in all the issues. Rather, the forms of participatory democracy are seen as necessarily operating alongside Congress, legislatures, and city councils. The opportunity for direct participation in consequential deliberations is seen as being available to all the people, when they choose, on issues that are important enough to them to warrant such an expenditure of time and energy.

Searching for Alternatives

What then are the potential realities of participatory democracy? What are the major possibilities and obstacles for community-based organizations in such a democracy? To examine this potential, we first have to reach a clear understanding of how participatory organizations operate, and how they differ from the representative model. Elements of representative democracy and participatory democracy operate side by side today in many American jurisdictions. So intertwined have they become that we often fail to recognize the very different structural models that lie behind these two approaches to popular rule.

In the strictly representative model, the lines of authority and legitimacy are rather simply drawn. Citizens choose their representatives —whether councillor or congressperson, mayor or president—and these representatives in turn are in charge of making policy and supervising the administration of government. An organizational chart of society would show "the public" in the role of a board of directors, at the top of the pyramid, in complete control.

But this is the static picture. When the element of time is added, the role of the public in the representative model becomes much more sharply limited. Unlike a board of directors, which retains its actual control through decisions made at regular meetings, the active role of the public is exercised exclusively by casting votes for candidates on election day. For a smaller segment of the population, this role is slightly broadened to debating the merits or demerits of particular candidates with their fellow citizens a few evenings before the election. In the time between elections, citizens are relegated to a passive role: watching how the government performs and, as the next election rolls around, listening to opposing candidates for office.

In the strictly participatory model, the organizational chart is more complex. The box labeled "the public" remains at the top of the hierarchical pyramid. But instead of neat lines from citizens to their elected officials, new elements are added. These include decision-making bodies open to broad segments of the public—ideally, bodies open to all citizens, on an equal footing. Those who choose to be involved become, to varying degrees, community decision makers. In any community larger than a few thousand people, there must be many such bodies, each small enough to retain the opportunity for face-to-face interaction of all participants on a regular basis. These bodies in turn interact with specific elements of government appropriate to their concerns, from the highest to the lowest policymaking and administrative levels.

Unlike the representative model, the participatory model is not confined to a narrow time period. Yet the dynamics of the participatory model are also relatively simple: it is a steady-state model—the public is expected to be involved to the same degree at all times. In both theory and practice, the role of the public is much more like that of the board of directors, meeting regularly to exert influence throughout the development and implementation of a policy.

Of course, in practice, neither model holds strictly to form. In a practical representative process, citizens do not limit their political activity to a few days once every four years. Public interest and special interest groups of infinite variety form to propose and oppose policy changes, and to lobby all levels of the governmental hierarchy, from the mayor to the line administrator to the public themselves. These groups might be seen as identical to the organizations of the participatory model, but they differ in three fundamental ways. First, most tend to be relatively hierarchical internally, run by a core of people who initiated the organization, with a very limited role beyond financial contributions for the average member. Second, most are not open to all community members, but only to a small segment who share the interests—often financial interests—of the originators. Finally, taken together, these organizations greatly overrepresent a very small elite within the population, generally those with the greatest economic resources.[9]

Similarly, participatory models may diverge widely from the norm. None exists independently of a representative structure. The relationship of the participatory bodies to that structure is often only vaguely defined. Their powers and influence vary widely depending on issues and political circumstances, particularly on issues that are seen as critical to the well-being of the whole city. Contrary to the steady-state assumptions of the model, citizen interest varies dramatically with the changing relevance of these issues, and inevitably, added participation provisions are needed when this interest peaks. In addition, the same interest groups that affect representative politics are interwoven within the participatory structures.

Characteristics of the Participatory Model

Our purpose in this book is to compare a segment of real-life American citizen organizations with the participatory model, and examine the potential of these organizations to fulfill that model. Throughout this analysis we will need to keep in mind three components that are its essence:

1. The Core. Small, face-to-face decision-making bodies are the fundamental structures of any participatory endeavor. Without them, much of the vital human interaction that creates community is lost. Many such bodies, thoroughly networked, are presumably necessary in any large polity to provide access to all citizens. One of their fundamental missions is to offer a welcoming forum to everyone within their jurisdiction, and to any issue they may choose to bring along. We will want to understand better what kinds of structures facilitate these missions, and what interactions are needed to make them function well for their community. We will also want to know how they can maintain themselves as a permanent part of our democracy.
2. The Link to the Community. Energetic outreach by the core groups is essential to keep participatory opportunity alive for all members of the community. Citizens need to know that such groups exist, what issues they are tackling at any given time, and how people like themselves can be involved. Over time, a reliable link will assure citizens that their voices will be heard and acted upon whenever important issues arise. How can all this be done? And how can these links overcome the participation gap between rich and poor, well-educated and poorly educated, overprivileged and underprivileged, that exists in all known forms of political action?
3. The Link to Government Policymaking. To create participatory democracy, the core groups must have political impact. Extensive interaction of these grassroots structures with the administrative and policymaking arms of government at all levels allows them to be effective on the issues that matter. Each group will make decisions and take positions on the issues. Most issues affect more than one community. We will want to learn how the individual group and its decisions can combine with others in

the larger community to reach conclusions appropriate to the scale of the problem—citywide, statewide, national, or even international. What works to combat parochialism, special interest domination, and cooptation? What is needed in reciprocal relationships with the representative elements of our democracy?

Recognizing "The People's" Interests

Chapter 2 delves into the nature of representation and its relationship to participation and the aggregation of interests. This will help us chart our course toward strengthened democracy. Chapter 3 describes the empirical basis we will use to examine the potential for participatory democracy in America—a set of over 270 neighborhood organizations in four of the most participatory cities in the country. Chapters 4 through 6 compare the operations of these organizations within each of the three components of the participatory model: the core groups, their link to the community, and their link to the public policy process.

The four communities we have chosen for their strong participation structures are Birmingham, Dayton, Portland, and St. Paul.[10] In each, the key elements of face-to-face interaction are neighborhood associations. Citywide participation mechanisms are part of their participation systems as well, including committees and citywide advisory boards. But they would be isolated, rather meaningless tokens of participation without the neighborhood organizations and support networks that continuously renew the participation process.

Neighborhoods are geographically defined collections of people with common interests determined largely by their physical proximity to each other. Neighborhood associations address those common interests. Many other kinds of organizations exist in the community, the workplace, and the nation, and also help citizens strive for goals their members have in common. It will be my contention that community-based organizations are a necessary but not sufficient basis for the participatory structure of a modern society. As urban studies of neighborhood relationships have consistently shown,[11] a large share of an individual's personal interactions today in America occurs outside any small geographic area, and commonly extends to the metropolitan expanse, and to a lesser but increasing extent, to other parts of the country and the world. Coupled with evidence of the dramatic increase in number and power of broad-based interest groups during the last thirty years,[12] these interactions force the conclusion that other grassroots structures—which still meet the conditions of face-to-face decision making and the other criteria we will be examining in this book—are needed in parallel with the neighborhood-based process to move our democracy from a representative toward a participatory basis.

Our ultimate focus is on issues that transcend the neighborhood, the narrow interest group, the political party, or the workplace, yet our approach will be derived from participatory successes in each of these. And the structures examined here will be ones that have the potential to unite the impact of participation in these realms into a single policy result at the local, state, and national levels. Our intention is to try to understand the implications for each area, and each area's impact on the larger issues, based on the lessons we can learn from the neighborhood. For the lessons we have learned, in fact, go far beyond the boundaries of the neighborhoods to the heart of democracy itself.

Chapter 2

The Aggregation of Interests
Representation, Voting, Parties, and Interest Groups

A central tenet of this book is that our system of representation as now structured is faltering, and needs to be rejuvenated with new approaches to democratic governance. This argument, in essence, takes two forms. First, the practical application of representative government in our multilayered society of 250 million strays far from the basic principles of effective representation, as well as from its practice at our nation's founding. Second, the theory of representation itself is critically flawed in the context of the needs, abilities, and interests of citizens in modern American society.

To examine these propositions and their relationship to participatory democracy, we need to explore the range of meaning in the concept of representation and how it relates to existing mechanisms for aggregating interests in American society.

From Patriarch to Parliament to Participation

At the heart of effective governance, whether democratic or not, is the idea of representation. As the noted political philosopher J. Roland Pennock states in his extensive review of the nature of democracy:

All regimes gain legitimacy by being in some degree representative . . . or at least by convincing an effective majority (sufficient number) of their subjects that they are.

[T]he two main claims of monarchs and dictators from which their legitimacy appears to have derived were (1) that they stood for, gave expression to, and supported the interests (and ideals and aspirations) of their people; and (2) that they were in some fashion authorized to act (generally within variously stated or implied limits) in the people's behalf.[1]

Yet it is obvious that representation in a democracy means something more. We use the concept of democratic representation as a primary way of distinguishing modern democracies *from* dictatorships. A *body of representatives,* and not just a single person, however democratically elected, is an essential ingredient in this distinction. Just as, in moving from a monarchy to a democracy, the idea of representation develops and expands, so too is it likely to require further elaboration as we move from pure representative democracy to a more participatory form. But it is not to be shunned in a kind of Rousseauean reflex against all forms of representation in a participatory democracy. In a society larger than a few thousand people, a concept of representation remains vital to even the most participatory democracy we can devise.

Perhaps the most thorough recent examination of the concept of representation is that provided by Hanna Pitkin in her landmark 1967 work.[2] In looking at the way in which we use the word "representation," she identifies four major sociopolitical uses of the term:

1. As *authorization:* A representative is someone who has been authorized to act by another. The person(s) who authorized the representative are responsible for the consequences of the action as if they had taken the action themselves. The conduct of the representative is only limited by the bounds of the authority s/he has been given—that is, by the range of activities and issues on which s/he is authorized to act.
2. As *accountability:* A representative is one who will have to answer to another or others for what s/he does. In this view, there are no limits to what a representative can legitimately do, if s/he is willing to suffer the consequences (that is, not being reelected) when the time for accountability arrives.
3. As a symbolic *"standing for":* A body of representatives is supposed to reflect those it represents in all relevant characteristics: for instance, percentage of blacks, women, low income, and so on. The actions of the representative body are in no way constrained other than by the characteristics of those chosen to serve.
4. As a substantive *"acting-for"* that can take at least three distinct forms:[3]
   • Status of *trustee,* who controls resources but is obliged in his or her trust agreement to administer those resources for the benefit of an individual or group; its essence is "acting in the interest of."

- Status of a *delegate*, who is sent by another or others with explicit instructions to carry out a specific mission.
- Status of *agent*, in the way that a lawyer is an agent for his/her clients in court; this is a position somewhere between (yet distinct from) the concepts of a servant and an independent contractor; it is used in the sense of "acting in place of" or "substituting for." "Agency" also represents more of a range of meaning than the others.

Pitkin argues that each of these, alone, provides a reasonably defended but inadequate statement of representation used in political analysis today. I argue here that each of these characteristics has a value in illuminating the differences between representative and participatory approaches to governance.

The first three, for example, tell us nothing about the *obligations* of representatives in the job of representing their constituents, but define only how they are to be established (authorization version), terminated (accountability version), or descriptively defined (symbolic version). All are necessary but not sufficient considerations of the representative process.

Representation as authorization, discussed in great detail by Thomas Hobbes,[4] focuses on the ability of the representative to legitimately take binding and often far-reaching action. This is what A. Phillips Griffiths calls "ascriptive" representation, which, in his view, encompasses political representation.[5] But as Pennock notes, this approach places too much emphasis on powers of the representative, and not on his/her responsibilities.[6] A speech by my representative, for example, clearly does not commit me to her views. And, realistically, it is not the individual representative in most situations who has the power to commit his/her constituents, but rather the legislative body as a whole. Still, this view of representation embodies one critical concept: that the result of the representative's work should have real and direct impact upon government policy. This simple prescription, while almost taken for granted in most discussions of representative government, is all too often ignored when considering participatory processes. The assumption in the latter case is frequently that any representative role will be only advisory, or that the representative can only discuss issues and not enter into binding agreements at all. As a result, the role of a representative in a participatory framework is unnecessarily and substantially weakened. In this area, the participatory framework needs to more closely parallel the representative framework in order to be effective.

Representation as accountability suffers even more from a focus on power rather than on responsibility. Its value is particularly limited in this regard by the time lag between action and electoral reaction. Here, the participatory framework largely overcomes these disadvantages. Instead of waiting two, or four, or six years before accountability can be exercised, a participatory framework that includes regular face-to-face meetings of interested citizens with their representatives—on a monthly or even more frequent basis—assumes that the principle of accountability is applied at each such meeting. In many circumstances, the representative can be replaced on the spot. The motive may be dissatisfaction with performance as a representative, or simply the recognition of a need for new skills for future work.

Representation as symbolic standing-for is always problematic. Its sole value lies in circumstances where the characteristics of potential representatives—for example, in race, religion, gender, or age—are so critical to the issues to be discussed that a failure to reflect the constituents' characteristics ipso facto means a failure of adequate representation in one or more of the other senses of the word. In other circumstances it adds little value to the representative process. As Griffiths notes, no one would argue that lunatics should be represented by lunatics.[7] This does not differ between participatory and representative frameworks.

The fourth form of Pitkin's representation is the heart and soul of the concept for democratic governance. It is the only version that establishes criteria to evaluate whether the representative actually does a good job of representing his clients. The greatest controversy about the nature of representation is usually expressed as a dichotomy between the first two aspects of "acting for": representative as trustee versus representative as delegate, or alternately as "leadership versus responsiveness." In some ways, this issue touches upon a fundamental difference between representative and participatory perspectives. In other ways, it presents a false dichotomy.

On the most basic level, the two posited extremes of trusteeship and delegation are both unrealistic. No one would argue that a representative is or should be a pure trustee in the usual, nonpolitical sense of the word. For a trust is legally an ownership of property, given to the trustee on condition that it be used in specified ways for the benefit of another person. In most cases, a trustee is not required to consult the persons for whose benefit she holds the trust, and, in fact, those beneficiaries are often considered incapable of acting for themselves by reason of age or infirmity. A representative, on the other hand, is not given title to a property, and is expected to engage in some form of consultation. Even the most ardent advocate for representative as trustee acknowledges that this trusteeship must at least be coupled with the periodic accountability of that trustee through the electoral process. The participatory perspective, of course, differs more from the pure trustee model, but does not divorce it completely. For even here, a representative is given a range of powers "in trust" that they will be wisely used. The key understanding, however, is that a participatory body that chooses a representative takes on the power to define exactly how much that trust will be limited, and does so not once for the existence of the nation, nor even once every four years, but every time it meets and confirms or denies the powers of representation to its representative. Completely missing from the participatory perspective is the assumption that the beneficiaries, the representative's constituents, are in any way incapable of acting on their own on these issues. On the contrary, the explicit assumption is made that even when the representative is chosen for his or her unique political or technical acumen, the values to be applied to any policy decision are those of the constituents and not only of the representative.

Conversely, few of even the most ardent participatory advocates would argue that the representative is purely a delegate. The life of any political community, even at the local level and certainly at the state or national level, is much too complex to allow delegation to be the only form of political operation. Furthermore, citizens are in general not highly political animals. Few want to be actively involved in every issue that is raised in the political arena. But at the core of the participatory perspective is the concept that when citizens want to be involved in an issue they can be involved, and when explicit instructions are given to a representative on an issue, that representative is expected to follow those instructions to the letter. Depending upon the circumstances, representatives may have relatively few instructions on pending issues and therefore relatively great freedom of action, or they may have comprehensive instructions that sharply limit their flexibility. From the participatory perspective, the choice about the degree of limitation is up to the constituents themselves.

The final element of representation, in the form of agency, is both more complex and more realistic than either the trustee or delegate approach. The concept of a representative "substituting for" his/her constituents, acting in their place when they cannot be there to act themselves, is an important aspect of representation in any large democracy. Yet, as Pitkin points out, defining what we mean by "substituting for" is not easy. If you are my representative, I do not always want you to act as I would have acted. For example, if I designate you as my representative to straighten out my financial affairs because I tend to lose patience with numbers and throw up my hands in frustration, I don't want you to do the same thing in my place. From the perspective of representation as agency, the concepts of trusteeship and delegation both come into play. Agents are expected both to follow any instructions that have been given, and to act upon their best judgment within that framework for the benefit of their constituents. In this context, the issue of "trustee versus delegate" becomes one of how much discretion is to be allowed, a question that, from a participatory perspective, is to be determined by conscious choices of the constituents as discussed above.

The question of "leadership" is often raised by those who advocate that representatives should ignore the clear choices of their constituents and follow their own lights. From a participatory perspective, leadership is also important. But in this perspective leadership means persuasion, not self-aggrandizement. Instructions from constituents, however explicit and comprehensive, do not need to be accepted without comment. If a representative finds those instructions to be unwise, unfair, unjust, or otherwise repugnant to her own political vision, she usually has the means and opportunity to make that case to her constituents. By virtue of being chosen as a representative, she has the ear of those constituents. If she fails to make the case, and fails to convince the constituents, she then has the option of acceding to their demands, or stepping down in favor of a representative who will

Pitkin's resolution of the trustee/delegation issue is what I would term a "moderate representative" point of view that takes some from each of the extreme representative and participatory perspectives. She argues that we should be looking for a form of representation in politics that meets at least the following criteria:[8]

- "[R]epresenting here means acting in the interest of the represented, in a manner responsive to them."
- "The representative must act independently; his action must involve discretion and judgment; he must be the one who acts."
- "The represented must also be (conceived as) capable of independent action and judgment, not merely being taken care of."
- "And, despite the resulting potential for conflict between representative and represented about what is to be done, that conflict must not normally take place. The representative must act in such a way that there is no conflict, or if it occurs, an explanation is called for. He must not be found persistently at odds with the wishes of the represented without good reason in terms of their interest, and without a good explanation of why their wishes are not in accord with their interest."

The extreme representative point of view rejects the necessity of responsiveness, the assumption that constituents are always capable of independent action and judgment, and the assertion that the conflict must be avoided or explained. The participatory point of view rejects the assertion that a representative must always act independently (sometimes pure delegation is appropriate), and that explanation of a disagreement is necessarily adequate (sometimes the judgment of the representative must be overturned, or the representative replaced).

Representing More than One

Up to this point, all of this discussion could be applied to representation of a single person by another person. We have yet to consider the extensive complications that ensue from large-scale representation and the conflicts of interest and ideas internal to any large constituency and within the nation as a whole.

Pennock begins to address these issues by bringing in factors of local versus national constituencies and the impact of a party system, along with the trustee-versus-delegate dilemma, to an analysis of "theories of how representatives ought to act."[9] Any examination of the way a legislature works in practice, however, reveals many more pressures and concerns that are a daily part of the legislative process. These include at least the following influences (where "desire" is used to indicate expressed choices, and "interest" is used to indicate the representative's judgment of benefits for the constituency indicated):

- Desire of a majority of constituents
- Interest of a majority of constituents
- Intensity of desire of a faction of constituents
- Intensity of interest (need) of a faction of constituents
- Protection of minority interests and rights within constituency
- Each of the above, but with respect to the national population rather than the representative's local constituents
- Moral principles, as held by the representative
- Personal interests/desires of the representative
- Intensity (urgency) of personal interest of the representative
- Pressures from the legislative leadership and the need to compromise to achieve any legislative action
- Pressures from party leadership and the need to shape an image or gain resources for the party
- Personal friendship networks within the legislature and mutual back-scratching agreements for the benefit of any of the above.

I list these not as a prelude to a general theory of representation—the appropriate impact and practical power of each of these factors has been debated since representative democracy first came into being—but so that recognition of these influences can help to sharpen the distinctions between the representative and participatory perspectives on democratic structure and draw out additional propositions about the representative process.

Both representative and participatory perspectives agree on at least one overall goal of a democratic system: that policy decisions should be made for the greatest benefit for the greatest number within the appropriate constituency—decisions made in a local legislature should benefit the local constituency, and decisions made in a national legislature should benefit the national constituency. All the disagreement arises on how we get to that happy condition.

An immediate problem arises, for both perspectives, on the question of majority versus minority interests and desires. There is substantial disagreement in our democracy on even the most basic principles of majority rule. At one extreme is the position that the majority vote must, in practical terms, determine all issues of public policy, and that "minority rights" are mere legalistic fabrications, not worth the paper they are declared upon. Others argue that minority positions and interests must be able to win under specific circumstances and conditions. Lani Guinier, made famous by a tremendous conservative reaction over her nomination (and subsequent withdrawal) in 1993 by President Clinton for Chief of the Justice Department's Civil Rights Division, has proposed that the legislative process itself may need to be adjusted to help permanent minorities obtain an appropriate share of the benefits allocated by the political process.[10] Indeed, few would argue today that a desirable outcome is for any minority of citizens to remain permanently excluded from basic resources and benefits available to all others. For the purposes of this book, I will put forward the following proposition, recognizing that it is much easier to state than to find the practical means to fulfill:

All else being equal, any democratic system that yields policy decisions proportionately allocated to a majority and a consistent minority in accordance with their numbers is preferable to a system in which the majority always defeats the consistent minority.

A "consistent minority" here means a segment of the population or of their representatives that consistently votes in the same direction on a set of issues, a direction consistently in opposition to the votes of the remainder of the population or their representatives on that set of issues, over a period of several years or more.

In addition to broad propositions such as these, there are a number of important implications of the pressures on representative decision making listed above for the representative and participatory perspectives.

First, one of the primary justifications for the very existence of a legislature in a democratic system is that it can help sort through these conflicts more productively and fairly than can a single elected official. The give-and-take of a legislative process is supposed to be essential to this "sorting through." If this proposition has a degree of validity, and most democratic observers seem to believe that it does, is it not equally valid when applied to a single legislative district? For example, given the range and varying intensity of interests and desires that exist in nearly every congressional district in America, does not a congressional district assembly that can instruct its congressman on the best positions to take for that district share exactly the same justifications as the Congress itself in its role of instructing the president and his/her cabinet on the best positions to take for the country? We will leave this as a question for now and return to it later for some answers.

In addition, the last five items on the list of representative pressures—from personal interests to legislative back-scratching—all have no intrinsic relation to benefits for the representative's constituency. Yet all are strong components of legislative life, often denied or ignored by advocates of the representative perspective. From the participatory view, they each deserve constant monitoring by constituents themselves, and full explanations whenever suspicions are aroused. And their strength and pervasiveness present powerful arguments against the advocates of a pure trustee form of representation.

Finally, some analysts of representative democracy perceive a kind of "invisible hand" that allows representatives, whose only commitment need be to the parochial interests of their own constituency, to collectively arrive at decisions in the best interest of the nation as a whole. A more realistic perspective is that some degree of awareness and concern for the national interest itself is important in reaching such decisions. Yet whichever argument one accepts, a key assumption is being made: that in reaching their decision, legislators learn to accommodate interests other than those of their own constituency in order to permit action by the legislative body as a whole. This is an assumption that seems to be borne out in practice. Compromises are made. Bills pass. Legislators accept the results. What we often ignore, however—and in the current political climate, much to our own peril—is that in an ordinary legislative process the *constituents* are not brought along. They do not learn to accommodate other interests, nor recognize what compromises must be made to achieve action. An apparent result is a tendency for them to place all blame on the legislators or on the legislature as an institution for failing to meet their particular interests. Phenomenally low poll ratings of Congress and high dissatisfaction with incumbents in recent years seem to bear out this assessment. From a participatory perspective, representation advocates are reaping what they have sown. By failing to maintain the key links between citizens and their representatives, and failing to use the participation process as an educational tool for citizens to gain understanding of the differing political needs and aspirations of other citizens, the growth of alienation seems inevitable.

Having examined the broad features of representation itself, and considered the role of participatory processes within these features, we turn now to key elements of interest aggregation within the representative process and how they differ from the forms of participation we are considering here. These elements are voting, political parties, and interest groups.

Voting and Participation

Without voting, in one form or another, there is no democracy. Voting is so intertwined with our concept of democracy that some commentators have assumed it to be the only condition for democracy: if a country votes for its leaders, it must be a democracy; if not, it is not. Even among those who postulate consensus as the only true form of democracy, as Jane Mansbridge points out, an implicit vote is a necessary part of the process.[11] And to the degree that the consensus is false, a consensus-based process departs from the democratic values we have discussed.

While it is a fundamental basis for either a representative or participatory process, voting plays a very different role in each. The most obvious difference is the time frame it places around the citizen. In a pure representative process, the active role of citizens is limited to five minutes in the voting booth once every year or two. In a participatory process, voting is a final stage of a discussion, likely to occur several times on different issues during the course of a single meeting, and extended to meetings occurring on a frequent schedule—monthly, weekly, or even more often. Most citizens will not choose to participate that frequently, perhaps, but the opportunity is extended to any who wish to accept it.

Perhaps even more important is the range of issue choice allowed in a pure representative democracy compared with a participatory democracy. In the former, the only possible vote is for a candidate who is expected to make decisions on dozens if not hundreds of different issues during his term of office. Even ballot questions, which comprise a substantial extension to a purely representative democracy, allow votes on only a tiny fraction of the issues a representative is likely to face. Conversely, in a participatory democracy, votes arise on every issue that gains sufficient interest within the group for it to be added to that group's agenda.

The character of these votes is, consequently, very different. The votes in a participatory situation are likely to be highly specific and to cover a single issue or issue complex. With that vote, the citizen can be expected to perceive a specific end result, such as the construction of a building or the implementation of a recreational program to which she and her family will have access at a definite time. The vote for the candidate in a representative framework, however, is of necessity highly diffuse. No matter how single-issue the campaign, or how much of a mandate for a particular platform is claimed, in most situations most voters will compromise their preferences on a range of issues, distilling them into a single mark for candidate Q. The voter may have a clear vision of what he expects to result from that decision, but, as post-election polls inevitably show, any two voters for the same candidate are likely to possess diametrically opposing views on a whole range of issues. Even taking the case of two candidates with positions on three different issues, Robert Dahl demonstrates that a candidate could theoretically win 75 percent of the votes, even though each of his/her positions on the three issues is opposed by 75 percent of the voters.[12]

As different as voting is within representative and participatory contexts, there are strong parallels between the decision-making processes of the two approaches. In a previous work, two colleagues and I developed a table that illustrates these parallels as well as their different characters. This table is reproduced here as Table 2.1.[13] It takes the form of the "preconditions for a polyarchy," Dahl's model for a real-world democracy, in comparison to the equivalent preconditions for a participatory decision-making process.

As Table 2.1 illustrates, the decision-making process that takes place in a participatory context possesses many of the same characteristics as voting alone does in a traditional representative democracy. Key propositions regarding access to the agenda, information, equal weight for the choices of all who participate, and implementation of the decisions are essential to each process. It will be important for us to examine in later sections of this book the potential obstacles to fulfillment of these specifications in both the representative and participatory contexts, and the relative likelihoods that they can be met in practice.

One of the key differences defined by this table is that "summarizing and evaluating" in the participation process replace the simple tabulation of votes. A second difference is that the final policy choices of the participation process are the focus of implementation, rather than the orders of the officials elected in a representative process. A third is that a whole range of interelection decisions

Table 2.1 Conditions for Democracy

Dahl's Conditions	Participation Equivalents
Polyarchy is defined loosely as a political system in which the following conditions exist to a relatively high degree:	Participatory democracy is defined as a political system in which the following conditions exist to a relatively high degree:
1. Any member who perceives a set of alternatives, at least one of which he regards as preferable to any of the alternatives presently scheduled, can insert his preferred alternative(s) among those scheduled for voting.	1. Any citizen who perceives a set of alternatives, at least one of which he or she regards as preferable to any of the alternatives presently scheduled, can insert his or her preferred alternatives among those scheduled for the participation process.
2. All individuals possess identical information about the alternatives.	2. All individuals possess identical information about the alternatives.
3. Every member of the organization performs the acts we assume to constitute an expression of preference among the scheduled alternatives, e.g. voting.	3. Every citizen performs the acts we assume to constitute an expression of preference among the scheduled alternatives, e.g., takes part in the participation process.
4. In tabulating these expressions (votes), the weight assigned to the choice of each individual is identical.	4. In summarizing and evaluating these expressions, the weight assigned to the choice of each individual is identical.
5. The alternative with the greatest number of votes is declared the winning choice.	5. The alternative with the greatest support within the participation process is declared the winning choice.
6. Alternatives (leaders or policies) with the greatest number of votes displace any alternatives (leaders or policies) with fewer votes.	6. Alternative policies that receive the greatest support in the participation process displace any alternatives with lesser support.
7. The orders of elected officials are executed.	7. The chosen policies are implemented.
8. Either all interelection decisions are subordinate or executory to those arrived at during the election stage, i.e., elections are in a sense controlling; or new decisions during the interelection period are governed by the preceding seven conditions, operating, however, under rather different institutional circumstances; or both.	8. Either all implementation decisions are subordinate or executory to those arrived at during the participation process (i.e., the participation process is in a sense controlling); or new decisions during implementation period are governed by the preceding seven conditions; or both.

that must be tenuously tied to the election results in the representative process instead becomes an intrinsic part of the ongoing participation process itself. These differences are products of the timeliness of the participation process in comparison with elections, as well as of the more direct relationship participation has to policy outcomes, or both. Each of these will be important factors in discussions of the links between citizens and the participation structures, and those between the structures and the governmental process, in subsequent chapters of this book.

Parties and Participation

During the history of representative government, political parties have taken on reputations ranging from corrupt factions to cornerstones of the American system. The most common modern view is perhaps best summarized by Walter Dean Burnham:

Once upon a time party politics nourished and quickened the very life blood of American democracy. Competition between the two major parties was keen not only in Washington and in the state capitols but in counties and cities and towns . . . today we sorely miss the vigor, the combativeness, and the pervasiveness of the populist party spirit that once animated our political processes at every level of government. Of all the major institutions of American society, the parties seem to be the most resistant to reform and modernization. . . . The great political question of this bicentennial decade is whether the parties will continue to stagnate organizationally or will be superseded—or transformed.[14]

A number of themes run through any description of U.S. parties. The idea of translating the expectations of the public or the "popular will" into governmental policy and action is an oft-stated justification of party function. Likewise, the essential role of "aggregating the interests of the public" and "articulating the policy positions of the majority" has been ascribed again and again to the major parties. This role is partially explained by, and partially interwoven with, the vigorously defended idea of linkage. Norman Nie remarks:

Political parties . . . constituted a major linking institution binding the citizens to their leaders, leaders to the citizens, and leaders to one another. Parties, as the receptor and aggregator of both electoral and non-electoral participation, aided, in these ways, the conversion of the many conflicting demands and desires expressed in the participation of the citizenry to policies and governmental actions that were responsive at least to some, if not to all, of the citizens.[15]

Everett Ladd writes on the same subject:

The potential electorate of the United States (persons of voting age) now numbers about 150 million. There is no way so large a body can achieve the type of participation and control which democracy presupposes without a "linkage" institution that organizes and distills and translates. The party system retains exclusive custody of this core democratic function—of aggregating the preferences of the mass public for political leadership and policy choice, and converting what was incoherent and diffuse to specific, responsive public decisions.[16]

These concepts of translation, aggregation, and linkage have been further expanded and elaborated to include a central party role in "mediating" social conflicts, constraining the whims of elected officials, and "representing interests that might otherwise go unrecognized." Burnham, who has been cited as one of the leading figures raising the alarm about the "end of parties," states the case for the latter party role in unfettered terms:

political parties, with all their well-known human and structural shortcomings, are the only devices thus far invented by the wit of Western man which with some effectiveness can generate countervailing collective power on behalf of the many individually powerless against the relatively few who are individually—or organizationally—powerful. Their disappearance could only entail the unchallenged ascendancy of the latter unless new structures of collective power were developed to replace them.[17]

In many ways, these party roles sound like the very ones we have been considering for participatory processes. The key question is: Have American political parties ever actually performed these functions? Let us examine some of the key elements, following the lines Austin Ranney has outlined as necessary components of a strong, responsible party system.[18]

Do the parties attempt to develop a detailed, coherent program based upon what they perceive the public wants? While party policies as expressed in platforms and other policy documents attempt to be comprehensive and multi-issue, they are far from coherent in either the substance or process of their development. In general, they have failed to reach out to the average person to determine his or her needs and interests, or in any sense to "aggregate" all of these issues into a coherent whole that makes sense as a single "for or against" vote by the electorate. As Ladd himself admits, party notables—not party organizations or the party rank and file—have made party policy.[19] Parties have seldom made use of any of the well-known citizen participation techniques that might allow them to capture the intensity and diversity of citizen concern. Instead, an incredibly pressured platform-writing committee in the heat of "convention fever" attempts to write party policy in response to the demands of small groups of party elites. And to top it off, these platforms have only a marginal effect on real party policy when the election is over, either in the halls of Congress, the White House, or the state house.

Is there party agreement, discipline, and unity, as demanded by the "strong, responsible party" theory? Nie asserts, "Political parties have provided the mass public with two or more legitimate sets of relatively cohesive leaders who shared a common electoral fate," and notes that "entire sets" of leaders have been vulnerable and were, in fact, swept out as a group in such critical elections as 1832, 1860, 1896, and 1932.[20] And we can add to this list the stunning Republican victories of 1994. Yet examples of programmatic, structural, and organizational disunity abound. The split between southern and other Democrats, alliances drawn from both parties for and against such issues as gun control, environmental protection (especially in its early days), or tax loopholes for an endless variety of businesses, are clear cases of party cross-cutting. On still other issues, such as land and water questions before the Interior Committee, votes tend to split sharply by geography, regardless of party.

In addition, the national parties often have been little more than loose coalitions of state or local party groups centered on local personalities and "party bosses." Membership has never required more than a simple declaration of a voter's desire to join. And as Rossiter has observed, our parties have generally been "creatures of compromise . . . vast, gaudy, friendly umbrellas under which all Americans, whoever and wherever and however minded they may be, are invited to stand for the sake of being counted in the next election."[21]

It is apparent, therefore, that while the American two-party system in some instances can lead to superficial agreement on issues within each party, it incorporates a much greater tendency to individualism in candidate campaigns and independence of elected officials, with only a minor degree of constraint due to party affiliation.

Are the parties internally democratic, in any of the senses we have been considering? One has to look high and wide for any shred of evidence that they are. Few party members ever attend a party function, let alone participate in shaping party policy. A tiny fraction even of party activists and campaign workers ever touch a party platform or submit an issue to be considered for inclusion in it. And reforms advocated by such bodies as the American Political Science Association Committee on Political Parties, or the McGovern-Fraser Commission before McGovern's smashing electoral defeat, have gone nowhere. Perhaps even more important, most of the rewards that our political system gives to a party—coming solely through electoral victory—focus on the means to achieve that victory, not the means to achieve issue consensus. Any party function that does not clearly contribute to victory in the next election—particularly a function as complex, time-consuming, and filled with uncertainty as an intensive participation process—is likely to wither and atrophy very quickly as party attention turns to the winning edge.

Do U.S. parties offer a real policy difference? The answer seems to be, occasionally, yes, on a few hot-button issues of the day; but at most times and on most issues, no. A description of the strong forces in a two-party system, which tend to push both parties toward the center, have been forcefully argued by Anthony Downs.[22] Using a single-dimensional model based on the work of Harold Hotelling, Downs concludes that because of the overriding goal of seeking a majority of votes from the same population, any two-party democracy causes the two parties to converge toward the center in order to avoid being seen as extremists; tends to encourage parties to foster ambiguities between their positions, and requires, for stability, a substantial consensus on ideology among voters. While Downs's theories have been challenged on a number of grounds, particularly that of his use of a unidimensional scale in his calculations, many of the forces he identifies seem to be a significant part of American politics. Party reformers have often argued that the differences between parties need to be made more clear, but generally have failed to develop the means by which such differences could be maintained.

Are people voting for parties or individuals? There is certainly a strong case to be made for the role of party identification as a significant component of the vote. From Lazarsfeld's first panel studies in 1936 to the recent voter surveys presented in *The Changing American Voter*, a strong tendency for voters to keep to the party of their parents is revealed.[23] In more recent elections, fewer people express strong party identification, many more call themselves independents, and younger voters stray more often from the traditional family party, but the predictive value of party identification on the individual's vote still appears greater than that of any other individual characteristic that has been measured. Nevertheless, on an aggregate level, election outcome can rarely be predicted from knowledge of party identification alone. In many districts, Democrats and Republicans alternate frequently as victors, despite a relatively stable majority of party leanings on one side or the other. Short-term factors, issues, and events, unrelated to long-term party perceptions, are often the determining factors. And as party identification declines in strength, the impact of these short-term factors becomes even greater.

Once in office, do elected officials support their party's program? As the final link in the chain of responsible party government, the broad goals of program implementation are only as realizable as each of the links that led up to this point. If no coherent and realistic party programs are developed by either major party, no effective policy based on these programs can be implemented by the victorious organization. If party discipline is not strong, or if positions in different parts of government are filled by members of different parties, no unified action along party lines can be taken. If parties don't offer programs that are substantially different from one another, the evaluation of the results of these programs by the voters, and their subsequent approval or disapproval, have no intrinsic policy implications. The result of the 1994 Republican victory is an illustration of how unusual is the exception. The "Contract with America" highlighted differences from the Democrats, was at least superficially coherent, and engendered an amazing degree of party discipline both during the campaign and immediately afterward. Yet even then, the extent to which the planks of the Republican party platform of just two years before were overshadowed by the Contract, and otherwise almost completely forgotten by public and politician alike, is evidence of the more typical state of support for party programs. And, of course, the Contract itself languished largely unimplemented within a few years' time.

It is clear, then, that the ideals of responsible parties so glowingly described by Burnham, Nie, and Ladd, are far from the reality of modern political practice. It seems equally clear from both direct historical evidence and the conclusions of contemporary observers that such parties have never existed upon the American scene.[24] Yet many responsible party advocates would still insist that we ask whether such parties are possible in the future. By providing the impetus to strengthen, unify, and discipline each of our two major parties, or even to encourage realignment into two new parties, can we bring our political system closer to the responsible party ideal, and thus reduce the need to consider other, more participatory methods of interest aggregation?

There are a number of problems with this prospect. First, the parties are heavily dependent upon their environment. Austin Ranney makes a strong case that the formal governmental system of the United States, coupled with the belief structure concerning politics and political institutions that has developed in this country, have a determining effect on the nature of political party development.[25] He notes that federalism, separation of powers, fixed terms, staggered elections, the direct primary, and the electoral college system all lead toward a fragmented, decentralized, and broadly focused party system.

Second, it is clear that we cannot look to other countries as a model. Writers who have examined this question conclude that even a British-style system imported to America would fall short of the hopes of responsible party advocates, both because of its own failing on the criteria they advocate, and because of the enormous contrast between the relatively unified, small-scale parliamentary form of British government and the heterogeneous, multilayered, congressional form of American government.[26] The same lack of immediate applicability is largely true for nearly every multiparty model available internationally. If the concepts of responsible party government could be developed in this country, they would have to take an essentially new form, for which no other system can be an adequate guide to the results we might expect.

Third, it seems unlikely that any of the responsible party functions we considered could be transformed into something approaching the ideal of the responsible party advocates. It is hard to see our two-party system breaking free of the Downsian pressures to offer the middle road for any extended period of time. Party discipline will always run second to federalism and the separation of powers. And, as the dismal fate of the 1972 Democratic party reforms makes clear, the scope of internal reforms necessary to enable participatory linkage to the broad base of the party is likely to destroy the very nature of the party system. In fact, many responsible party advocates have admitted that the only form of linkage parties can realistically provide is that which occurs in the voting booth every few years. E. E. Schattschneider has conveyed this message most clearly:

The unfortunate result of the confusion created by the concept of the party as a large association of partisans is that it blackens the name of the parties. The parties are the most important instrumentalities of democratic government. To call them oligarchies and thus to identify them with undemocratic tendencies is unfortunate. If it is true that the democratization of parties is impossible, what is to be gained by insisting on it?

A more realistic theory, closer to the facts, can relieve us of the nightmarish necessity of doing the impossible. Let us suppose that the concept of the party membership of partisans is abandoned altogether. If the party is described as a political enterprise conducted by a group of working politicians *supported* by partisan voters who approve of the party but are merely partisans (not members of a fictitious association), the parties would seem less wicked."[27]

A "linkage" to the voter that consists of but a single choice every two years between alternatives produced by exactly two—no more, no less—private organizations called parties, is indeed a version of democracy that is commonly accepted. But is it really much more than the linkage between the consumer and MacDonalds or Burger King, providing for the choice between styles of fast-food hamburgers, while ignoring the fact that one may be looking for steak, lamb chops, or tofu?

Interest Groups, Social Movements, and Participation

Many observers have seen the development of interest groups and social movements as an important answer to the deficiencies of political party structure. Certainly they create a large number of opportunities for individuals to express many more shades of issue positions than is possible in a simple vote for a candidate or support of one of two major political parties (or even multiple parties in a typical parliamentary system). Yet, with the explosion of citizen groups during the last thirty years—at both the local and national levels, and everywhere in between—it has become clear that such groups also have significant shortcomings and thus fail to move us very far, as a society, toward a participatory democracy.

Up until the early 1960s, the study of social movements had taken three basic forms. The first might be called the bureaucratization approach, based primarily on the work of Max Weber and Roberto Michels. Michels formulated the now famous "iron law of oligarchy" whose essence is that "organization implies the tendency to oligarchy . . . (every group) becomes divided into a minority of directors and a majority of directed . . . where organization is stronger, we find that there is a lesser degree of applied democracy."[28] Weber emphasized the routinization of charisma: "It is the fate of charisma, whenever it comes into the permanent institutions of a community, to give way to powers of tradition or of rational socialization."[29] And Zald and Ash add the third concept of goal transformation: that, as an organization ages, goals become more diffuse and indefinite, and there occurs an "accommodation of organization goals to the dominant societal consensus."[30] Yet the variety and rapid changes visible in social movements of the last three decades make it clear that these principles apply only to certain types of social movement organizations under certain conditions at certain times in their development. Many stages of development within specific movements show tendencies exactly opposite to this bureaucratization approach. For example, as Jo Freeman points out, the women's liberation movement originated from a heavily bureaucratic mechanism of federal and state commissions on the status of women, developed through relatively centralized groups such as the National Organization for Women and the National Women's Political Caucus, and only later spawned the extremely decentralized, participatory, and even antibureaucratic branch encompassing innumerable small groups engaged in a wide variety of women's rights and service activities across the country.[31]

The second form of social movement investigation involved the extensive efforts of the collective behavior school of sociological research, based on the crowd behavior analysis of Gustave LeBon. A fundamental perspective of this approach is that social movements are only slightly more organized crowds, and that irrational behavior is a basic characteristic of many crowd actions. This form of analysis in large part represents deviant psychology applied to groups. In the late 1950s, Ralph H. Turner developed the widely accepted concept of *emergent norms:* "In crowd situations, the individual acts not because he or she is automatically infected by group emotion [as earlier collective behavior theorists had postulated], but rather because certain lines of behavior are seen as appropriate. New norms appear in an undefined context."[32] Neil Smelser, in his landmark book *The Theory of Collective Behavior,* developed six conditions that are postulated to be necessary and, together, sufficient for the occurrence of an "episode of collective behavior": precipitating incidents; strain or structural conflicts that generate conflict; conduciveness or susceptibility of the structure to change, generalized belief or exaggerated and unrealistic myths held by those seeking change; and social control or response by authorities to the efforts for change.[33] The existence of Smelser's "generalized beliefs" in a wide range of social movements has been challenged by a number of authors.[34] A strong case has repeatedly been made that irrational beliefs or norms are no more inherent in many social movement organizations than in the social institution they seek to change, or in the reaction of authorities to the social movement.

A third form of social movement analysis stems from the study of political interest groups. The groundwork for this analysis was laid by Arthur Bentley, who argued that "there are no political phenomena except group phenomena," and that "there is no group without its interest."[35] David Truman elaborated upon the concept of the primacy of pressure groups, and extended it with the idea that unorganized "potential interest groups" were necessary to explain "such ideals or traditions as constitutionalism, civil liberties, representative responsibility, and the like."[36] From this conceptual base grew the major controversies between the "pluralists" led by Robert Dahl and the "power elite" theorists led by C. Wright Mills, which focused on the degree to which major pressure groups were responsible for controlling public policy. A host of community power studies have attempted to identify specific actors and processes involved in local decision making. Yet most of these studies have been restricted either to well-established, well-funded, and typically bureaucratized organizations, or to social/military/political elites, and have generally ignored the potential impact and dynamics of emerging organizations and loosely structured movements. The politics of the 1960s proved how inadequate this approach was. As James Q. Wilson points out, not only did large-scale, rapidly changing movements and "mass politics" take center stage in the public arena, but the increased importance of public-opinion polling and television led many to conclude that direct candidate interaction with the electorate was becoming as significant as, or more significant than, indirect contact through pressure groups.[37] Ironically, the brief success of taking the "Contract With America" directly to the public in the 1994 elections may have brought this process full circle: it bypassed interest groups and the traditional lobbying pressures to dramatically boost the political fortunes of one of the major political parties.

Recognizing the inadequacies of the existing theoretical approaches, a number of scholars in the 1970s and 1980s began to develop a new perspective on interest groups and social movements: using the theoretical framework of resource mobilization. This new approach focuses on specific organizational forms, social supports and constraints, strategic dilemmas, social control, and the interplay of external supports, elites, and oppositions. It identifies the necessary conditions and resources for the development of social movement organizations, and examines the dynamics of their interaction.

Anthony Oberschall most effectively describes the concepts involved:

> The basic idea is that of resource. This can be anything from material resources—jobs, income, savings, and the right to material goods and services—to nonmaterial resources—authority, moral commitment, trust, friendship, skills, habits of industry, and so on. In ordinary everyday activity, at work, in family life, and in politics, people manage their resources in complex ways: they exchange some resources for other resources; they make up resource deficits by borrowing resources; they recall their earlier investments. Resources are constantly being created, consumed, transferred, assembled, and reallocated, exchanged, and even lost. At any given time some resources are earmarked for group ends and group use, not just individual use.
>
> Mobilization refers to the processes by which a discontented group assembles and invests resources for the pursuit of group goals. Social control refers to the same processes, but from the point of view of the incumbents or the group that is being challenged. Groups locked in conflict are in competition for some of the same resources as each seeks to squeeze more resources from initially uncommitted third parties. When one party to the conflict succeeds in obtaining some hitherto unallocated resources, these resources are no longer available to the opposition.[38]

The central feature of this theoretical framework is the birth, growth, decay, and transformation of social movements and social movement organizations. In many ways, resource mobilization incorporates the strengths, and rejects many of the weaknesses, of the earlier theories as they were applied to these movements. Zald and Ash, for example, examine the application of the Weber and Michels bureaucratization approach, and are able to specify conditions under which bureaucratization is most likely to occur and conditions under which it is unlikely.[39] Second, the use of demonstrations and an understanding of crowd behavior are important factors in resource mobilization from the point of view of social movement leaders and opposition authorities alike. Yet, as Edward Walsh points out, most social movement analysts now reject the distinction between routine and extreme politics, and no longer assume that the discontented who unite to attain social change goals necessarily act any more or less rationally than other political actors.[40] Finally, while resource mobilization recognizes the importance of ongoing, established groups using traditional political tactics to influence government policy, it provides a framework in which these groups are seen as only one part of larger social movements. In this context, emerging and decaying social movements that may possess no recognizable pressure group in the pluralist sense can be understood.

Taken together, these wide-ranging forms of analysis point out four major problems interest groups and social movement organizations have in meeting the conditions for a participatory democracy: legitimacy, cacophony, inclusion, and repertoire.

Legitimacy. One of the most crucial questions involves the issue of who is represented by individual interest groups, and by interest groups in the aggregate. In defending the pluralist perspective in the mid-1950s, Robert Dahl claimed that the American political system had evolved to a point at which "all the active and legitimate groups in the population can make themselves heard at some crucial stage in the process of decision."[41] In light of the subsequent experiences of the 1960s, 1970s, and 1980s, when a vast number of individuals and groups have made it quite clear that they felt their voices were not being heard, few analysts today can take this statement seriously. Most would agree with Schattschneider's poignant critique: "The flaw in the pluralist heaven is that the heavenly chorus sings with a strong upper-class accent. Probably about 90 percent of the people cannot get into the pressure system."[42]

But the problem is not just one of income or class; even in communities with some strong low-income organizations, only a few of the many otherwise excluded voices are brought into the political system. After all, most citizen groups, from national economic-interest groups to grassroots community groups, are organized to advance the particular interests of a narrowly defined constituency. They do not have the internal structure or the motivation to balance all interests in the community or the nation. There are no guidelines, no process, no structure, and certainly no "invisible hand" ensuring that anything like a balance is obtained. As a consequence, it is very hard to argue that the collection of interest groups and social movements existing at any time actually *represents,* in any of the senses we outlined, the public as a whole or the interests of the public as a whole.

In addition, political jurisdictions and organizational membership are often not well aligned. Many organizations achieve success either by organizing a small number of people from many communities into a powerful voice or by taking dramatic action within a community to focus attention on a previously neglected minority. As Heather Booth notes: "With our organizations, if we have an active participation of 3 percent of the community, we can feel like a majority. In an election, unless you get out the vote of 50 percent plus one of those voting, you end up as a loser."[43] The point is not that effective participatory democracy is beyond the capability of existing community groups, but that its measures of success are very different from those that many existing organizations normally use.

Cacophony. In addition to the potentially wild imbalance of interests pressing on the decision-making process, their cumulative interaction often leads observers and participants alike to reject the whole process as untenable. Lowi, for example, considers this problem as leading to a complete blockage of effective governance:

Interest-group liberal solutions to the problem of power provide the system with stability by spreading a *sense* of representation at the expense of genuine flexibility, at the expense of democratic forms, and ultimately at the expense of legitimacy . . . [This "new representation"] impairs the potential of positive law to correct itself by allowing the law to become anything that eventually bargains itself out as acceptable to the bargainers . . . In a pluralist government there is, therefore, no substance. Neither is there procedure. There is only process.[44]

It is the negative impact of this cacophony of interest group voices that has led many political observers to look back longingly to a strong party system as a primary aggregator of interests. The perceived impossibility of managing a multitude of independently expressed interests is perhaps most dramatically expressed by E. E. Schattschneider:

The people are a sovereign whose vocabulary is limited to two words, "Yes" and "No." This sovereign, moreover, can speak only when spoken to. As interlocutors of the people, the parties frame the question and elicit the answers. To say this is not to disparage democracy; it merely demonstrates that parties are made possible by nature's limitations on the behavior of large numbers of people.[45]

Yet if we seek to allow people more than a two-word vocabulary, and if parties have indeed failed in the role of enabling participatory democracy, we need to continue the search for other alternatives that can turn the cacophony into the heavenly chorus *sans* such ruinous accents.

Inclusion. Many interest groups and social movement organizations possess and are possessed by a clear mission. They have no interest in bringing in people who do not agree with that mission. Their role is to advocate their position before some more powerful body, and let the chips fall where they may. Other groups, particularly those whose primary mission is to "organize" one specific community, see themselves as the ultimate in inclusivity within that community. Their degree of success in this inclusiveness varies a great deal in practice, but they have in common a large exclusive tendency: namely, toward people in any other community whose interests may be different from their own. Even if such organizations have the will to extend their reach, they often run into problems in the attempt. This is particularly true when the potential constituents are looking for different kinds of incentives: some beneficiary (material-oriented), some solidary (friendship-oriented), and some purposive (accomplishment or value fulfillment). As McCarthy and Zald argue, "A social movement organization which attempts to link both conscience [purposive] and beneficiary constituents to the organization through federated chapter structures, and hence solidary incentives, is likely to have high levels of tension and conflict."[46] Their argument continues, "The more unlike one another workers [active constituents] are, the less likely there is to be organizational unity, and the more likely it is that separate clique structures will form." A major objective of the analysis, therefore, is to discover ways in which this tendency to self-destruct in the face of internal conflicts can be overcome.

Repertoire. The character and traditions of many organizations reduce their capacity to be participatory organizations. The tactics, internal structure, and external relationships necessary to be successful in a larger political framework often undercut any participatory inclinations they may have. The repertoire of any organization is necessarily restricted. As Charles Tilly observed:

At any point in time, the repertoire of collective actions available to a population is surprisingly limited. Surprisingly, given the innumerable ways in which people could, in principle, deploy their resources in pursuit of common ends. Surprisingly, given the many ways real groups have pursued their own common ends at one time or another.[47]

From the perspective of many citizen groups, particularly Alinsky-type[48] community organizations, the nature of electoral action is very strange indeed. For the rules of the game are determined not by the citizen group, in good Alinsky style, but by outside forces heavily draped in tradition and legalistic structure. Many members of social movement organizations look upon politics as "dirty" and beneath the efforts of a pure and uncompromised citizen organization. Politicians are seen as a bunch of crooks—or at least slippery fast-talkers out for their own personal interests above all else. And the game of politics often leads to a partisan splitting of forces over personalities instead of the unity to which any good organizer aspires. As Heather Booth noted when the Citizen Action organizations across the country first considered becoming involved in electoral campaigns: "electoral politics are traditionally controlled by other people's political parties. It is hard to build both your own organization and support a party's candidate . . . you can't even control the fights with your allies. . . . In some ways choosing candidates can create divisions we might not otherwise face."[49]

And it is clear that the leaders of an organization cannot simply adopt a new political tactic and expect the membership to go along without objection. As Zald and Ash point out, many social movements fail because they become discredited by the use of tactics or acceptance of outside support that is viewed as illegitimate by their supporters.[50]

The ultimate argument that something more is needed—something beyond interest groups and social movement organizations as they have existed during the last three decades—is that they have not brought us visibly closer to a participatory democracy. In fact, despite a tremendous growth in the number and acceptance of such groups within the political arena, citizens have felt less and less represented or involved in political decisions during this time. No dramatic new developments are underway within the electoral process, political parties, or advocacy group movements that seem to offer much hope for changes on the scale needed to reshape our democracy. We need to look at other models for an answer.

Chapter 3

Participatory Alternatives
The Neighborhood Approach

> Where the state is the only environment in which we can live communal lives, they inevitably lose contact, become detached, and thus society disintegrates. A nation can be maintained only if, between the state and the individual, there is intercalated a whole series of secondary groups near enough to the individuals to attract them strongly in their spheres of action and drag them in this way into the general torrent of social life.
> —Emile Durkheim

To develop alternatives to pure representative democracy, we need to examine the building blocks and networks that make participatory, face-to-face interaction possible. The smallest unit in the network clearly needs to accommodate all who want to be involved and allow them to work with each other productively. One kind of group that meets this criterion is the neighborhood organization. We will delve into the detailed requirements that such an organization should satisfy in the following three chapters. In this chapter, we will lay the groundwork for that examination by describing the neighborhood structures that are part of this study, and the data that has been gathered on their activities.

Neighborhood organizations have been the subject of a great deal of literature in the social sciences, but most work has focused on the concept of neighborhood itself, on neighborhood change, or on the social interactions that do or do not take place at this level. For many, the only political role of neighborhoods has been a reactive one in response to racial and other "destabilizing" pressures of change. Juliet Saltman has classified this literature into three basic perspectives:[1] the traditional "degenerative theory" of neighborhood change, which postulates a standard pattern of decay following low-income racial or ethnic migration to the area, described by Wilson[2] and Molotock;[3] an "interactionist" theory, which argues that social support networks can prevent this kind of decay, based on the work of Suttles[4] and Hunter;[5] and an "interventionist" theory growing in the 1980s, which states that racially integrated neighborhoods will stabilize if sufficient resources are mobilized for collective action early enough. Leading advocates of the latter include Orfield,[6] Taub,[7] and Saltman[8] herself. A major version of this line of thought, expressing a kind of historical determinism in the form of a five-stage "neighborhood life cycle," has been advanced by Downs,[9] and has become widely accepted. Naparstek[10] and Cohen,[11] however, have offered serious critiques of this view.

Another vast body of neighborhood research has focused on the desirability of a kind of village life that neighborhoods may or may not be able to provide. This work began with assertions by researchers such as Wirth,[12] Nisbet,[13] and Stein[14] that urban neighborhoods cannot duplicate the functions of the small village community that we all know and love. Others, however, such as Janowitz,[15] Jacobs,[16] Gans,[17] and Fischer[18] have pointed out that many people remain involved in their neighborhoods, have significant numbers of attachments there, and even use neighborhood interaction as a guide to social behavior.

The perspective of this book differs from that of most neighborhood research in that it attempts to look at neighborhoods in an organizational framework tied into, or potentially tied into, the larger political reality. While many of the issues that neighborhoods in this study do become involved with, particularly in the area of zoning and land use, reflect the kind of pressures for neighborhood change considered in the foregoing literature, the vast majority of the organizations are not in a reactive mode. Their neighborhoods are not threatened by daunting social forces. For the most part, in fact, these neighborhoods are relatively stable. And they are working on issues that encompass the whole range of quality of life in an urban setting.

In addition, our understanding of these organizations is not limited by the extent to which village-like communities are a reality in their neighborhoods. While the social interaction that takes place in the neighborhood, within the organization itself and between the organization and the community at large, is important to this study, the focus here is upon those forms of interaction that have relevance to the political issues of concern to neighborhood residents. Some of these issues may be very local and "village-oriented," but many others involve problems that ultimately must be dealt with at city, state, and even national levels. The question for this book is how well such organizations, springing from a community setting, can deal with the full range of political issues our society faces.

Constructing a Neighborhoods Reference Source

The neighborhoods we chose to examine were in four geographically and demographically diverse cities that have some of the most comprehensive neighborhood-based participation systems in the country: Birmingham, Alabama; Dayton, Ohio; Portland, Oregon; and St. Paul, Minnesota.[19] Citizens in each city have built a network of neighborhoods that cover nearly all of the city's population, and their organizations are recognized by most government bodies as important community voices.

Birmingham has a three-tiered system with an extensive neighborhood structure including officers elected every two years at the polls, neighborhood coalitions called "communities" that regularly bring together the neighborhood officers, and a citywide Citizens Advisory Board with representatives from every community in the city. Each association communicates with all households in its neighborhood through a monthly newsletter, decides how its community development block grant allocations will be used, and is assisted by the city's community resource staff in finding solutions to neighborhood issues. It was this neighborhood structure that first brought the city's blacks and whites together in any community endeavor, after more than a decade of some of the most severe racial turmoil in the country.

Dayton's neighborhoods are linked together by seven Priority Boards whose members are either elected by precinct through the use of mail ballots, or sent directly as representatives of the neighborhood groups. The neighborhoods and the city have established an extensive two-way communication and decision-making system. It includes: leadership training; a monthly "administrative council" in which representatives from every major city agency are held accountable before each Priority Board; regular use of neighborhood needs statements as part of the annual budget process; regular public opinion polls about city services; and a wide range of neighborhood-oriented planning, initiatives, and self-help programs. In addition to the day-to-day issues of land use, housing, environmental protection, and crime prevention, the neighborhoods have had a major impact on long-term citywide initiatives, from bond issues to education reform.

Portland neighborhood associations, added one by one to the neighborhood system over the course of twenty-five years, contract with the city through seven District Coalition Boards to provide "citizen participation services" to the city. Each coalition, made up entirely of representatives of neighborhoods in its section of the city, hires and fires its own staff, works out of its own neighborhood offices, raises additional funds beyond the $1.2 million provided by the city (in the 1986–87 fiscal year), and coordinates activities with a central Office of Neighborhood Associations at city hall. The structures consciously balance coalition advocacy, neighborhood needs reports, crime prevention teams, and individual neighborhood issues, with a range of citywide initiatives including budget advisory committees for every major city agency, comprehensive neighborhood planning, self-help development grants, and a citizen mediation program.

St. Paul chose to organize using a smaller number of larger neighborhoods, each centered on an elected District Council. Consequently, each Council is able to have its own neighborhood office and staff, with some funds provided by the city and other funds raised by the Council itself. The councils have substantial powers, including jurisdiction over zoning, ability to shape the delivery of a range of city services, and a central role at all stages of the city's capital budgeting process. Community centers, economic development efforts, crime prevention programs, an early notification system for all major city agencies, and a district newspaper in nearly every council area help to make the system one of the most coherent and comprehensive of any city in the country.

Details of each city's neighborhood system are provided in Appendix B. In each city, this research effort included two major public opinion surveys with initial samples of nearly 1,100 citizens per city; tracking of issues reaching the public agenda over a two-year period; and in-depth personal interviews with the mayor and city councillors, major city department heads, leaders of the neighborhood coalitions, and officers of a wide range of independent citizen groups working on issues affected by city policy. A detailed analysis of this data on an individual level is provided in *The Rebirth of Urban Democracy*.[20] The purpose of this book is to look at this data from a neighborhood-level perspective and attempt to understand its implications for a participatory democracy.

Table 3.1 outlines the participation structures as they exist in each city. Taken together, these four cities had a total of 273 recognized neighborhood organizations that covered 94 to 100 percent of the population in each city. The information about each of these neighborhoods and their organizations was obtained from three types of sources.

The first set of information was obtained from the public opinion polls themselves. These surveys were stratified by neighborhood to the maximum extent possible. The specific methodology varied with the information resources available in each city. We were able to obtain individual names and addresses sorted by neighborhood from the city of Birmingham, for example, but only received approximate geographic boundaries of phone-prefix information

ᴉle 3.1 Participation Structure and Resources

	Birmingham	Dayton	Portland	St. Paul
ᴊ population	288,611	193,536	375,897	270,230
ᴉghborhood associations				
nber	93	73	90	17
ᴡest population	180	11	70	7,000
dian population	2,740	1,830	4,250	15,800
ᴊhest population	8,200	10,300	13,800	26,000
ᴉ Tier	22 communities	7 priority boards	7 district coalition boards	None
ᴊwide citizen body	Citizens Advisory Board (CAB)	Priority Board Chairpersons Meeting & CDBG Task Force	Budget Advisory Committees (BACs)	Capital Improvement Budget Committee (CIB)
ghborhood and				
ᴉistrict staff	None	24	26	32
ᴊwide staff	9	4	11	1
ticipation budget				
ᴊrom the city	$500,000	$1,200,000	$1,200,000	$486,000

ᴇ:
figures reflect the status of the participation system in 1986–87.

from the St. Paul telephone company. Regardless of the stratification method, running logs of neighborhood identification were kept to help us reach a target quota in as many neighborhoods as possible. In addition to this initial neighborhood identification, each respondent was asked for the street intersection nearest to his or her home.

The second set of information was obtained from U.S. census data. Each city is a participant in the Neighborhood Statistics Program, in which the Census Bureau provides detailed statistics for the city broken down by the neighborhood areas defined by the city itself, in addition to the usual census-tract breakdowns. While this data allows us to establish very accurate demographic characteristics for the defined neighborhoods, there are several sources of gaps in the data: first, neighborhoods that have been redefined since 1980 (a particular problem in Dayton, where all neighborhood boundaries and definitions were reviewed in 1985–86); second, neighborhoods added to the city or the neighborhood system since the 1980 census (this was especially a difficulty in Portland, where a major annexation process was underway during the time of this research); third, neighborhoods that were so small that privacy issues required the Census Bureau to lump several together for reporting purposes.

The third set of information about the neighborhoods was obtained from in-person and phone interviews of neighborhood leaders and coalition staff. In most cases the respondent was the staff person most directly concerned with providing support services to a specific group of neighborhoods. We asked for a range of data indicating levels of neighborhood activity and participation during the 1985–87 period. In some cases, as a result of recent changes in neighborhood boundaries or organizations, this information was not available. In addition, the type of information varied significantly from one city to another, corresponding to widely varying community activities and responsibilities at the neighborhood level.

Table 3.2 indicates the extent of neighborhood coverage we were able to obtain in these efforts. The first column shows the total number of neighborhood organizations existing in the city at the time of the initial survey. In parentheses is a percentage indicating the proportion of the city's total population represented by these organizations. A striking feature of these cities is the extremely high percentage of neighborhood representation they have been able to attain. The second column of this table describes the number of these neighborhoods that had useable economic information from the Neighborhood Statistics program in the 1980 census, and the corresponding population covered by these neighborhoods. Again, the coverage is over 95 percent in each city. While several major changes in neighborhood definition did occur between 1980 and

Table 3.2 Neighborhood Coverage

	Total number of neighborhood associations		Neighborhoods with available census data		Neighborhoods available for strength rating	
Birmingham	93	(97.6%)	82	(96.0%)	81	(93.8%)
Dayton	73	(99.1%)	61	(97.4%)	59	(95.5%)
Portland	90	(94.9%)	71	(97.0%)	84	(92.4%)
St. Paul	17	(100%)	16	(98.8%)	16	(98.8%)

Notes:

All figures in parentheses represent the percentage of the city's population living in the neighborhoods indicated.

1. In St. Paul, one district is split into three separate organizations, but all statistics are calculated on the combined district population.

2. Portland was undergoing a large scale annexation at the time of our study. In some cases, census data was available for areas without recognized neighborhood associations.

3. Dayton had undertaken a major review of neighborhood boundaries during the course of our study. Our figures are based on the earlier version of the boundaries, consistent with the 1980 census data.

4. In all cities, the downtown core neighborhood was excluded from our statistical consideration.

1987—including large-scale annexation in Portland and a complete review of neighborhood boundaries in Dayton—the system in each city was stable enough to provide a solid basis for this research. The neighborhoods enumerated in the final column required information both from the neighborhood leaders on organizational activity and from individual survey respondents living in that neighborhood. Much of our analysis will require both the census and respondent data, reducing the number of neighborhoods available for analysis but still allowing us to reflect at least 90 percent of the population of each city.

Neighborhood Organization Strength

What constitutes a strong, effective, and highly participatory neighborhood organization? There are many ways to answer this question. Most of the research dealing with the political role of neighborhood groups has consisted of community case studies of from one to less than half a dozen neighborhoods. As such, they have often taken the strength of the organization they are working with as a given and gone on to describe the role it has played in community issues. But several broader studies have found that coalitions of neighborhoods are sometimes effective in dealing with large urban bureaucracies,[21] that neighborhood associations help to equalize the distribution of services,[22] that specific neighborhood structures are important in meeting citizen needs and building citizen trust.[23] Others have been able to conclude that those who participate in local volunteer organizations are more likely to be involved in informal social interactions in the neighborhood,[24] and that a lack of organized neighborhood groups can add to disjointedness of local politics and undermine the authority of the mayor.[25] Only a few authors have attempted to develop a mechanism for evaluating or comparing neighborhood organizations, as Wandersman has done as a means of helping block organizations to maintain and strengthen themselves,[26] or as Yates has done in an attempt to evaluate organizational democracy.[27]

The large number of neighborhoods that this study attempts to include in its analysis meant that this research could not do the kind of in-depth examination of social relationships within each neighborhood that a single case study is able to accomplish. Yet this study is able to provide much more connection between public opinion results and neighborhood-level analysis than most surveys can attain. It was concluded that the most useful comparisons of neighborhood organizations in this context would come from the summation of as many small elements of neighborhood activity as possible. In the end, we settled upon twenty-one measures of activity, as listed in Table 3.3. As that table indicates, each city had a characteristic pattern of availability of this information, and for some items, particularly in Birmingham, the uniformity of operations was sufficient to render the item of little use to distinguish between levels of neighborhood activity.

We have grouped these twenty-one measures into three key elements of neighborhood strength. *Core Activity* is an indication of how energetic is the cadre of activists who hold the organization together. This can range from having no cadre, no meetings, and no visible activity to having a core group that meets frequently, raises funds to carry out its projects, and takes every opportunity available in the city to have an impact on its political environment.

Table 3.3 Availability of Neighborhood Organizational Strength Data

	(Value range)	B	D	P	SP
A. Core Activity					
1. Organization has current officers	(0/1)	+	+	+	+
2. Elections held for officers within past two years	(0/1)	*	+	+	+
3. Organization regularly sends representative to larger coalition body	(0/1)	*	+	+	+
4. Produced neighborhood needs report at least once in last two years	(0/1)		+		
5. Frequency of regular meetings (number held in two years)	(0–48)	+	+	+	+
6. Have non-profit corporation status	(0/1)		+		
7. Annual operating budget	(0–98,000)	+	+	+	+
8. Staff size	(.5–5.0)				+
9. Spend all of annual city appropriations	(0/1)		+		
10. Significant local fundraising	(0/1)				+
B. Outreach					
1. Frequency of newsletter production (number in two years)	(0–28)	*	+	+	+
2. Percentage of households reached with average newsletter	(0–100)	*	+	+	+
3. Number of newsletters which reach all households (over two years)	(0–28)	*	+	+	+
4. Percentage of average newsletter content contributed by organization	(0–100)	+		+	
5. Scope of special projects during last two years (rating)	(1–5)	+	+	+	+
6. Special outreach efforts conducted during last two years	(0/1)			+	
C. Involvement					
1. Average attendance at regular meetings	(0–100)	+	+	+	+
2. Average attendance for special projects	(0–2500)	+	+	+	+
3. Average attendance at annual meetings	(0–225)			+	
4. Number of active block clubs or crime watch groups (rating)	(0–5)	+			+
5. Number of active project organizers (volunteers)	(0–200)		+		

Notes:

+ = Data is available that distinguishes between neighborhoods.

* = Data is available but is essentially uniform for all neighborhoods in that city.

Outreach represents the level of effort made by the organization to keep its community informed and bring in new people to work on organizational projects. This outreach can take the form of canvassing the neighborhood door-to-door, developing presentations for cable television or other media outlets, conducting phone campaigns, sending out newsletters, putting up posters, holding public events, and so on. One of the most consistent measures of outreach we found in these neighborhoods involved the frequency and coverage of newsletters and other reports distributed on a household-by-household basis.

Involvement measures the level of actual community participation in the meetings, events, and activities of the organization. This can range from a handful of people running everything to the active involvement of a significant percentage of the neighborhood, either as participants in neighborhood events or as active volunteers. In many ways this is the most important characteristic of a strong neighborhood group, but it also presents the greatest difficulty in obtaining reliable information from the available sources.

The elements for each of these measures were combined into a scale with possible values from zero to six for each city. Appendix C provides details of scale construction. Each scale is applied uniformly within each city and, to the extent possible, uses comparable items for each increment between cities. For example, a neighborhood in Portland ranks highest on the Core Activity Scale if it has elected officers during both of the last two years, if it has sent in neighborhood need requests to city departments each year, if it regularly sends representatives to the district coalition board, if its annual budget is at least $1.00 per neighborhood resident, and if it has held neighborhood meetings more than 36 times in two years. A neighborhood of 6,000 in St. Paul ranks highest on the Involvement Scale if it typically has more than 25 people attending its bimonthly meetings, has more than 85 attending its annual meeting, has more than 500 at special events, and has organized virtually the entire neighborhood into block clubs (120 of them).

Table 3.4 illustrates the level of several activities typically carried out by the neighborhood organizations in these cities. Each value in the table reflects the percentage of neighborhoods in that city that attain a fairly high level of activity on the specific measure indicated. It is clear that the St. Paul structure, with its larger neighborhoods enabling at least a part-time staff person to be working for every group, has characteristics that set it apart from the other cities. These organizations are able to maintain a schedule of meeting, event, and outreach activities on a more regular basis than the smaller groups in the other cities. On the other hand, on most measures of neighborhood participation (such as the special-event item used in Table 3.4), as a percentage of the neighborhood

Table 3.4 Neighborhood Strength Examples

Activity	Percentage of neighborhoods conducting activity			
	Birmingham	Dayton	Portland	St. Paul
Regular meetings 24 times or more in two years	65	42	34	100
Special events during each year attract over 20% of the neighborhood's residents	39	49	13	12
Produces substantial communications reaching every household in the neighborhood at least 4 times per year	20	18	34	71
Carries out a wide range of special projects, events, and advocacy activities over a two-year period	41	41	43	82
Has an annual budget of over $.50 per neighborhood resident	18	27	30	100

Note:
All figures represent the percentage of neighborhoods in that city which successfully conducted the indicated activity during the two-year period prior to our research effort.

population, it falls short. This is our first brush with a principle that we will encounter time and time again during the course of this investigation: that the size of the smallest unit in a representative system is a critical determinant of the system's characteristics (with both positive and negative implications for strong democracy).

The three basic scales were then combined into a single rating of neighborhood organizational strength, as described in Appendix D. Cut points were determined for each scale based on the range of activities and ratings in each city. The final strength rating has a value from one to five. A value of one indicates that the neighborhood scored among the lowest in the city on all three basic scales. Such an organization barely exists, limping along with little or no visible activity. A value of five indicates that the neighborhood scored among the highest in the city on all three basic scales. These neighborhoods tended to show consistently active leadership, extensive outreach, and high levels of neighborhood involvement in meetings and events. Intermediate values reflect a mixture of high and low scores on the three basic scales, or a moderate rating on all three scales. A summary of the results of this process is given in Table 3.5.

There were a few neighborhood organizations that did not fit well into this analysis of activities and operations. Upon further examination, the expected levels of participation—specifically in terms of the "participation difference" (PD) results developed below—were sharply out of line with neighborhood strength indications we have been discussing. A ratings value of 7 or 8 was used to designate these neighborhoods. These exceptions fall into a total of five groupings of two to four neighborhoods each. Two groupings are in Birmingham, one consisting of outlying, high-income, heavily white neighborhoods with unusually low PD results (designated as a "type 7"); the other low- to moderate-income, heavily black neighborhoods bordering on the urban core and having exceptionally high PD results (designated as a "type 8"). Two are in Dayton, with characteristics strikingly similar to the Birmingham pair. And the remaining grouping is in Portland, consisting largely of moderate- to high-income neighborhoods that border on the city limits or a college campus, and which generate unusually high PD results in spite of almost nonexistent neighborhood organizations (another "type 8"). We will return to these pattern-breaking groupings of neighborhoods from time to time when they can provide illuminating sidelights to the general rule.

And the general rule is that the rating system based on organizational characteristics is highly correlated with the individual-level participation measures identified through our public opinion polls. Table 3.6 shows the basic pattern, which holds city-by-city as well as in the combined four-city results. Each figure represents the percentage of survey respondents in each category who had participated in the neighborhood system within the past two years. They range from a low of 11.1 percent of the sample in Dayton neighborhoods with the lowest organizational strength rating, to a high of 37.0 percent in Birmingham neighborhoods with the highest neighborhood strength rating. The chi-square value for each city is significant at least beyond the 5 percent level.

Table 3.5 Summary of Neighborhood Organizational Strength Index

	Number of neighborhoods in each strength category			
Index value	Birmingham	Dayton	Portland	St. Paul
Low 1	7	13	18	2
2	21	10	19	4
3	29	16	19	3
4	13	10	17	5
High 5	5	4	7	2
Exceptions				
7	3	4	0	0
8	3	2	4	0

Note:
Each figure represents the number of neighborhoods in the indicated category of neighborhood organizational strength.

Table 3.6 Participation by Neighborhood Strength

Neighborhood strength index value	Percentage of respondents who participated (of N cases)			
	Birmingham	Dayton	Portland	St. Paul
Low 1	20.0% (30)	11.1% (81)	15.1% (106)	17.7% (79)
2	17.9 (162)	14.8 (115)	13.9 (144)	14.5 (228)
3	23.0 (230)	16.3 (172)	18.0 (194)	15.4 (136)
4	26.4 (106)	24.9 (185)	32.7 (110)	24.9 (189)
High 5	37.0 (27)	31.6 (19)	36.6 (41)	35.6 (87)
Exceptions				
7	5.7 (35)	11.4 (35)		
8	58.8 (17)	33.3 (9)	42.9 (28)	
Chi-Square	24.63	14.23	30.20	22.17
Significance	.000	.027	.000	.000

Combined results: percentage who participated, all four cities

Low 1	15.2%	(296)
2	15.3	(649)
3	18.7	(732)
4	26.6	(590)
High 5	35.6	(174)
Chi-Square	55.48	
Significance	Better than .01	

Notes:
Each percentage figure represents the proportion of survey respondents in that category who had participated in the city's neighborhood system during the previous two years.

The figure in parentheses represents the total number of survey respondents in that category.

The uniformity and strength of these correlations provides a compelling validation for the neighborhood rating scale. A strong link exists between the objective rating criteria and the self-reported participation of the public respondents. In every city, nearly twice as many people report that they participate in the neighborhood system in the highest-rated neighborhoods compared to those in the lowest-rated neighborhoods, and in Dayton this ratio is nearly three to one.

We still must ask, however, if this correlation is just an artifact of demographics, either on an individual or a neighborhood level. In the *Rebirth of Urban Democracy* we found a high degree of correlation between socioeconomic status and participation in virtually every measure we used. If the neighborhoods ranking low on organizational strength were the same ones where most of the city's low-income population lived, the rating system may not be measuring what we expect.

The first test of this possibility involves neighborhood-level data derived from the federal census. Using four economic measures of the neighborhoods—

median household income, percentage unemployed, percentage below poverty, and percentage receiving public assistance—in addition to two education measures—percentage graduating from high school and percentage graduating from college—we constructed a ten-point scale of neighborhood socioeconomic level. (See Appendix E). Table 3.7 shows the number of neighborhoods in the sample at each position on this scale. The general range is from lowest income and education to highest income and education, but two scale positions deserve a special note: the seventh scale position represents neighborhoods with a median position on most income measures but a college education level at least two standard deviations above the norm; and the tenth scale position represents neighborhoods with an exceptionally high income level—at least three standard deviations above the norm. Neighborhoods at these two scale positions may yield some interesting results as we go along.

How much of a difference do these socioeconomic factors make on participation levels? Table 3.8 shows the results for the four-city combination data. The chi-square value for this table is significant at beyond the .01 level, but there is little indication of a pattern of association from low to high levels of economic status. We must conclude that, contrary to the large impact of individual-level socioeconomic status, neighborhood demographics makes little consistent difference in participation activity. We will use these values of neighborhood socioeconomic status as a control for participation/neighborhood rating

Table 3.7 Summary of Neighborhood Socioeconomic Index

Neighborhood socioeconomic category	Index value	Number of neighborhoods in each socioeconomic category — Number of neighborhoods from four cities
Very low income	1	16
Low income, low education	2	27
Low income, moderate education	3	13
Moderate income, low education	4	12
Moderate income, moderate education	5	70
Moderate income, high education	6	9
Moderate income, very high education	7	6
High income, moderate education	8	38
High income, high education	9	31
Very high income	10	8

Note:

The terms very low, low, moderate, high, and very high roughly represent values for income or education measures which are −2, −1, 0, +1, and +2 standard deviations from the four-city mean of that measure. See Appendix E for the detailed breakdown of economic measures used to construct this scale.

Table 3.8 Participation by Neighborhood Socioeconomic Status

Neighborhood socioeconomic index value	Percentage who participated	Number of cases
1 Low income, low education	28.0%	75
2	19.9	221
3	13.7	102
4	19.3	83
5	16.6	1014
6	27.3	110
7	29.9	87
8	14.9	502
9	28.6	532
10 High income, high education	33.3	30

Note:
Each percentage figure represents the proportion of survey respondents in that category who had participated in the city's neighborhood system during the previous two years.

relationship a little later, but first we want to make one final refinement of the participation data.

Up to this point we have used an absolute measure of participation: the total percentage of people who participate within a given neighborhood. But socioeconomic status (SES) has a dramatic effect on a person's likelihood of participating under almost any external conditions. This effect could overwhelm any attempts to measure participation as a function of other variables. To refine our understanding of the impact of these variables upon participation, a measure can be constructed to incorporate the individual SES values into a participation prediction score for that individual. In essence, the measure predicts the likelihood that an individual will participate, based on the known demographic characteristics for that individual. For any grouping of individuals, it will tell us how many people are likely to participate in that group, if only individual-level socioeconomic factors are at work. The difference between this measure and the actual participation rate for the group will be recorded as the "Participation Difference" (PD) value that we mentioned earlier. A negative PD value implies that factors other than individual socioeconomic characteristics have led to lower participation than we would expect. A positive PD value implies that these non-socioeconomic factors have led to higher participation levels than we would otherwise expect.

To construct the participation prediction scale, we used six factors that our research team previously found to be significantly correlated with high participation levels: individual income, education, age, race, home ownership, and length of residency at the current address.[28] These were entered in a stepwise regression, with participation level as the dependent variable. A final multiple R value of .31 was obtained on the final regression step. The full regression equation and tables are given in Appendix F. This equation then can then be used to predict the likelihood that a particular individual will be a neighborhood participant, and, as described in Appendix F, to generate the Participation Difference result for any neighborhood or other grouping of respondents.

Using this Participation Difference measure, we can further test the validity of our neighborhood rating criteria. Table 3.9 lists the mean values of PD for each neighborhood strength group within each city and in the aggregate. As expected, PD values are generally negative for neighborhoods lower on the neighborhood strength scale, indicating that factors are at work in these neighborhoods that, independent of SES characteristics of the respondents, tend to lower participation levels in these areas. And PD values are strongly positive in

Table 3.9 Participation Difference (PD) by Neighborhood Strength

Neighborhood strength index value	PD value (of N cases)							
	Birmingham		Dayton		Portland		St. Paul	
Low 1	2.93	(30)	−3.31	(81)	−2.71	(106)	−4.13	(79)
2	−1.51	(162)	−1.92	(115)	−3.19	(144)	−2.39	(228)
3	4.17	(230)	−0.88	(172)	.07	(194)	−1.43	(136)
4	6.93	(106)	8.89	(185)	12.90	(110)	3.43	(189)
High 5	15.17	(27)	11.92	(19)	15.73	(41)	10.73	(87)
Exceptions								
7	−14.47	(35)	−9.96	(35)				
8	37.21	(17)	16.62	(9)	19.62	(28)		
Pearson's r:	0.87		.130		.154		.112	
Significance:	<.05		<.01		<.01		<.01	
Combined results: four cities PD (N)								
Low 1	−2.68	(296)						
2	−2.27	(649)						
3	.86	(732)						
4	7.53	(590)						
High 5	12.73	(174)						
Pearson's r:	.119							
Significance:	<.01							

Note:
Each PD value represents the average difference for survey respondents in that category between the "predicted" and actual participation levels. See Appendix F for calculation of the PD value.

The figure in parentheses represents the total number of survey respondents in that category.

Table 3.10 Participation Difference (PD) by Neighborhood Socioeconomic Status

Neighborhood socioeconomic index value	PD index	Number of cases
1 Low income, low education	11.1198	75
2	3.4537	221
3	−2.8548	102
4	4.6352	83
5	−.3564	1014
6	10.3090	110
7	7.8326	87
8	−2.8485	502
9	6.5188	532
10 High income, high education	5.8016	30
Pearson's r:	.0083	
Significance: Not significant at .05 level		

Note:
Each PD value represents the average difference for survey respondents in that category between the predicted and actual participation levels.

neighborhoods higher on the neighborhood strength scale, indicating positive participation factors at work. The high degree of correlation between neighborhood organizational strength and levels of participation is thus not impaired by this extensive control for individual socioeconomic status. Pearson's r is significant at better than the .01 level in every case except Birmingham, where it is significant at the .05 level.

Even with these individual-level controls, it may still be true that people who live in poor neighborhoods participate at different rates than those who live in rich neighborhoods, in a way that affects the neighborhood rating results. Table 3.10 shows that the PD values do indeed vary with neighborhood socioeconomic status, but again without a discernable directional pattern. Pearson's r is only .0083, not significant. And running a final partial correlation of PD with neighborhood organizational strength, controlling for neighborhood economic level, yields a strong .1313 value for the correlation coefficient, significant at well below the .01 level, confirming that the neighborhood strength measure remains important in generating higher participation levels after all controls are in place.

We thus have developed a database of 273 neighborhoods in four cities to use as a basis for evaluating the central propositions about face-to-face participatory democracy. For each neighborhood, we have available the full set of survey and personal interview results, as well as three new tools: a reasonable measure of neighborhood organizational strength, a measure of degree of participation beyond expected values (PD) that can be applied to a neighborhood sample of any size, and a census-based measure of neighborhood economic status. And we know that this measure of neighborhood strength strongly correlates with participation levels, independent of either individual or neighborhood socioeconomic factors. In the next three chapters, we use this measure to test other aspects of the neighborhood participation systems in the four cities of this study, and to explore how well organizations of this type can serve as a basis for participatory democracy.

Chapter 4

The Participatory Core

The first question we need to ask about the practical development of participatory democracy is: What is required of an organization at the core of this democracy? Specifically, for the neighborhood organizations on which this book centers, how well do the existing neighborhood groups meet these requirements? And, in charting our course for the future, what is necessary to improve the effectiveness of these organizations in this role? Can other kinds of organizations do it better?

In this chapter we focus on goals, structures, procedures, and interactions within the organization, and among those who choose to participate in it. In later chapters we consider two other elements of these core organizations: their grassroots community base and their political and policy impact.

Our earlier discussion of participatory representation, with its focus on the traditional structures of voting, political parties, and advocacy groups, leads us to examine five propositions about the internal requirements for the core groups of a participatory democracy. These propositions focus on equal representation, multi-issue capability, deliberation, openness, and maintenance of the core organizations. We will consider each in terms of its derivation from the strengths and weaknesses of traditional representation, the degree to which each requirement is met by the neighborhood groups in the study, and the changes or alternatives necessary to fulfill these criteria more completely.

Communitywide Representation

> *To the maximum extent possible, the network of participation organizations should represent every segment of the community on an equal footing.*

One person, one vote. This basic principle is a key attribute of the electoral process that gives elections legitimacy in our democracy. As we saw in Chapter 2, it is one of Dahl's basic conditions for a polyarchy—expressed in terms of the identical weight of every individual's choice, at every stage within the democratic process. It is the principle by which political parties measure their effectiveness. Ultimately, they win if they get more individuals supporting them than their opponents, they lose if they don't—no matter how many intervening factors, such as money and the media, help or hinder their efforts.

Yet the flip side is often overlooked. This same principle dramatically undercuts the legitimacy of advocacy groups. Since an individual can be a member of as many groups as she chooses, since the strength of an organization bears only a marginal relationship to the number of people who hold its point of view, since many points of view are almost completely unrepresented, and since there is no way to assure any kind of balance between the weight of advocacy group pressure on a particular issue and the actual level of support among the public, interest group advocacy is a shaky foundation on which to build a democracy. Lobbying more often comes under attack for subverting the representative process than for embodying it. Political leaders have enormous leeway to attack a high-profile lobbying campaign as "just another special interest," or laud it as the "voice of the people;" to ignore a "silent majority" or to take up its presumed point of view as a *cause célèbre*.

This problem is at the core of representation—whether it be traditional or participatory. We concluded from our analysis in Chapter 2 that a key element of representation is "acting in the interests of the represented in a manner responsive to them," and yet the representative "must be the one who acts." There are three key elements to these concepts:

1. someone making a decision (acting);
2. someone assessing the interests of a constituency and using that as the basis for his/her part of the decision; and
3. someone being responsive to actual people within that constituency.

By "acting," here, we clearly cannot mean actually carrying out the policy (the role of citizens in policy implementation will be considered in Chapter 6). "Acting" is used in the sense of making a decision that will be implemented because it is seen as a legitimate actionable decision. The administrators who have the resources to implement the decision owe their allegiance to these decision makers, they expect to receive instructions in this form, and they are committed to carrying them out.

Where is the locus of that decision? In a monarchy, the locus is abundantly clear: the king ultimately makes all decisions. He may delegate ministers to make subordinate decisions, but always with the proviso that he can take back the prerogative to actually decide any specific case at any time. In a democracy, it becomes substantially more complex. In our democracy, the executive, judicial, and legislative branches all make legitimate and binding decisions within certain frameworks that have become reasonably well defined. In all cases the population as a whole is seen as ultimately responsible for the decisions, but by much more circuitous routes than are available to a king: by election of the single authoritative individual in the executive case, by election of members of a group in the legislative case, and, in the judicial case, by election or by appointment and confirmation, combining the normal operations of the other two branches.

Only in the case of the executive is the decision still seen as residing within a single mind, that of the president, governor, or mayor, for example. In all other situations, the decision is not that of individual choice, but of collective choice by a legislative or judicial body, within an elaborately delineated process. Within certain bounds, the executive decision is seen as legitimate simply by being made, assuming the process of electing that person was seen as legitimate in the first place. A collective decision, on the other hand, must meet two conditions of legitimacy: first, each member of the collective must be seen as legitimately elected to the role s/he will play; second, the process itself must be seen as democratic. If, for example, one representative is able to consistently dominate the legislative process at the expense of the interests of all other representatives, through intimidation, bribery, or other maneuvers seen as illegitimate, any decisions that ensue from the body are under suspicion. (A host of political pressures, legislative/executive interrelationships, and advisory structures blur the boundaries between individual and collective decisions, of course, but this essential difference remains.)

The second and third elements—assessing the constituency's interests, and being responsive to the individuals represented—also imply a balance between all interests in the community. Just as a legislature attempts to balance the interests of all districts by providing equal votes to each district representative and providing equal access by each member to the body as a whole (that is, ability to introduce legislation, speak to the assembled group, serve on working committees, and so on—conditioned, in practice, by a host of seniority and power-brokering considerations), it is assumed that each representative is able to hear and balance all interests within her district. Each constituent has a right to expect that he will be given a hearing by the representative on a basis equal to that of every other constituent in that district.

Thus, a representative democracy inherently embodies an important principle also essential for a participatory democracy: that there exists a critical process of *interest identification, deliberation, and decision making in a collective body* that goes above and beyond the considerations required for the decision of a single individual. We will deal with other implications of this principle when discussing the internal democracy of a participatory organization in a later section, but there are two primary implications that are essential here: each party to the process should in some way be endowed with a share of legitimacy equal to that of all other parties, and the collective that makes the decision should in some way reflect all relevant interests within that community.

When the community is a city, these conditions can be met in any of three obvious ways: first, the decision maker(s) can be selected by all residents of the city; next, each decision maker in a collective body can be selected by residents of a district defined by the city in a way that preserves the principle of one person, one vote, or, finally, each decision maker in a collective body can be selected by democratic organizations in a way that preserves the principle of one person, one vote. The first two represent the traditional politics of the mayor and city council. The third approach is the subject of this discussion.

Neighborhood associations are a leading candidate for such democratic organizations. Because they are geographically defined, they tend to fit together to cover all community members on an exclusive many-to-one basis: that is, every citizen has one organization representing her/him, and no citizen has more than one organization representing her/him. Of course, in most American cities today, neighborhood groups do not in fact cover all of the city. Even among those cities in our larger survey[1] which have relatively strong neighborhood-based participation programs, it was found that 20 to 40 percent coverage of the city was considered to represent a high level of successful organization by many administrators and citizens involved. But the step to full coverage is well within practical possibilities, as is evidenced in each of the four cities making up our current study. As we noted in Chapter 3, each of the four have an organized network of groups that covers at least 94 percent of their population. And these groups are recognized as important advocates of the neighborhood, even in those neighborhoods with the weakest organizations. Table 4.1 shows the results of the public opinion survey question regarding how good the neighborhood association is in "letting the city government know what the needs of your neighborhood are." In every type of neighborhood, at least 55 percent of the respondents put the neighborhood associations in the highest of the three categories of response. This shows a slight but significant variation with the index of neighborhood strength. When neighborhoods were grouped into two categories—low organizational strength (index values 1 and 2), and high organizational strength (index values 3, 4, and 5)—the relationship is a little clearer. In the low-strength category, an average of 58.0 percent of the respondents felt the neighborhoods did a good job, compared to 64.3 percent in the high-strength category (significant at better than the .05 level).

In every city that we have examined, many other kinds of citizen organizations abound. In the four cities, strong advocacy groups existed on issues of the environment, human services, shelter for the homeless, labor, utilities and nuclear power, taxes, abortion, child care, youth services, recreation, and many more, as well as social/service/issue organizations with specific ethnic, religious, racial, and gender affiliations. In many instances, it is clear that these groups more closely reflect the specific issue positions of their members than the neighborhood associations reflect the positions of their constituents. The memberships of the former are relatively homogeneous on the issues central to the organization; the constituencies of the neighborhood associations are of necessity heterogeneous on virtually every issue that comes before them.

Yet this strength of the advocacy organizations in representing their members is also the weakness of a democratic system based upon them. Many who hold opposing views simply may not have organizations in their community to represent them. For example, we found no organization in St. Paul opposing city spending for more homeless shelters, no organization in Portland supporting nuclear power, and no organization in Dayton advocating for constriction of welfare benefits, even though public opinion polls revealed significant support for such positions. The opposite side on each of these issues had strong organizational advocates.

This disparity does not prevent a participatory system based on advocacy organizations, but it does complicate the situation. To establish such a system, and preserve the principle of one person, one vote, we would need to reach a social consensus about ways to allocate one's vote to an organization (or representative) on a nongeographic basis. The most comprehensive attempt to construct such an allocation is probably that presented by G. D. H. Cole in the 1920s. The heart of his system, based on a series of producer and consumer guilds, is that "man should have as many distinct and separately exercised votes as he has distinct social purposes or interests."[2] Unfortunately, one of the clearest lessons from Cole's work is the complexity that such a system would entail. A community would need to develop a substantial consensus on the areas that deserve independent representation—the workplace, for example, or the environment—and ensure that every person is represented by one and only one organization. For the workplace, factories and offices are obvious units,

Table 4.1 Citizen Evaluation of Neighborhood Associations

Neighborhood strength index value	Good job	Fair or poor job	(N)
Low 1	62.0%	38.0%	(121)
2	55.6	44.4	(313)
3	64.8	35.2	(372)
4	62.4	37.6	(338)
High 5	72.5	27.5	(102)

Pearson Chi-Square: 11.53 with 4 degrees of freedom.
Significance: .021

Notes:
Each figure represents the percentage of respondents answering the question detailed below.

Full question wording: Now let me ask if you think the Neighborhood Association does a good job, a fair job, or a poor job of letting the city government know what the needs of your neighborhood are?

but those who work at home as independent consultants or contractors, or have multiple jobs, also need to weigh in with "one and only one" vote. For an issue like the environment, each citizen would need to be presented with an opportunity to sign up with exactly one organization (or individual) as his/her "primary" environmental representative at any time, with the recognition that these representatives would be empowered collectively to make authoritative decisions on these issues, and that failing to choose such a representative would be equivalent to failing to vote on these issues.

In spite of the many non-neighborhood community organizations in each of the four cities of this study, the neighborhood groups were seen as among the most representative of the community as a whole. After our research team had asked about each respondent's affiliations with citizen groups and the neighborhood-based participation system, we specifically addressed this issue with the question: "Do you feel there is any group or organization that represents your community's interests better than the neighborhood association?" Overall, 87.6 percent said no. And of those who said yes, when asked an open-ended follow-up question about which organization better represents their community's interests, the answers ranged widely, with no identifiable pattern of a more representative group. This solid support of the neighborhood associations did not vary significantly by individual socioeconomic status, neighborhood association strength, or neighborhood economic status.

A Problem of Size

In spite of their coverage and their perceived representativeness, the neighborhood organizations we saw have a significant problem in meeting the one-person, one-vote criterion: the neighborhoods tend to vary dramatically in population size. Even in St. Paul, which has the least variation, the neighborhood with the largest population is twice the size of the median, and the smallest is half the size of the median. In the other cities, the largest neighborhood is three to six times the median for that city, and because in each city some very small neighborhoods are part of the system, the smallest is a tiny fraction of the median size. The Supreme Court would have a field day trying to apply redistricting standards here!

If we are to take the principle of one person, one vote seriously, and all that we have said about representation suggests strongly that we must, we have only two solutions: reconstruct neighborhood boundaries so that the populations are more equal (much as Congressional district boundaries are reconstructed after every census), or provide for a process that aggregates the interests of neighborhood groups in a way that weights final decisions by population.

The former is a recipe for disaster. In each of these cities, where neighborhood-based participation worked quite well, one cardinal rule was observed: the neighborhoods were natural groupings of people and geography. In Birmingham, staff from the community development department literally started at one end of the city and sampled households on a door-to-door basis, asking what people felt was "their neighborhood" and "their community." In Portland, each neighborhood group, as it organized, told the city what it wanted its boundaries to be—even when they overlapped the boundaries of other previously organized neighborhoods. In other cities, the process was less systematic, but the results were the same: the neighborhoods, large or small, were determined by a grassroots sense of what boundaries they were comfortable with. This process clearly helped to provide a sense of ownership of the organization and what it was trying to do. And a sense of ownership of the process is a large factor in what makes the process feel democratic to people. Compare this sense to the way that people feel about their Congressional District. In many cases, these snake through urban and rural areas with only a shred of contiguity providing any rationale for their composition. Consultation with citizens about what the Congressional District boundaries "should be" is almost universally nonexistent in the political process of congressional redistricting. Few citizens are even aware of all the cities and towns that are included in "their" district.

If we accept a grassroots method of determining neighborhood, we are left with the second alternative to achieve a one-person, one-vote outcome: weighting. Two basic approaches seem possible: allocating actual "votes" in any multi-neighborhood deliberation according to neighborhood population; or grouping neighborhoods together into larger units that do have roughly equal populations and equal votes. The first tends to run into a host of practical difficulties when individuals who serve as representatives from a neighborhood before a larger body have vastly unequal influence; the second is constrained by the artificiality of the grouping and by the necessity in most cases, of having small and large neighborhoods together in the same group. This creates the same weighting problem inside that group that we are trying to solve for the larger collective.

Each of the cities in the study faced this problem, but none of them faced it squarely. In Birmingham, Dayton, and Portland, larger bodies, called variously "communities," "priority boards," and "district coalitions," have populations more nearly equal than the neighborhoods. And in St. Paul, as we have noted, the populations of the district councils, the smallest unit in the participation system, are larger and less dramatically divergent in size. The variations in size of these larger units can still be more than two to one, or even greater in the case of Birmingham. In addition, dramatic variations in size of the neighborhoods within the larger units are almost universally ignored, except in Dayton. In this city, an added feature helps to even out the neighborhood variations. The majority of priority board members are elected directly from voting precincts of roughly equal population. The cost, of course, is that the neighborhood groups are bypassed in this portion of the priority board representation.

None of these anomalies seems to severely affect citizen confidence in the legitimacy of neighborhood representation. Our research team asked specifically whether any groups of people or neighborhoods "always seem to be treated better" or "always seem to be treated worse" than everyone else by city government. Table 4.2 shows the results. A little more than one-third of the respondents answered "yes" to this question, and the results show no significant variation by the strength of the neighborhood organization. For those who did answer "yes," the most common response was either "those groups which are better organized" or "the rich" get treated better, and "those who are not organized" or "the poor" get treated worse. The economic class implications are amplified when we examine these results by neighborhood socioeconomic status. As Table 4.3 indicates, the "some are treated worse" responses range from 43.1 percent for low-income neighborhoods to 33.6 percent for high-income neighborhoods, significant at better than the .01 level. Still, even for those in the lowest-income neighborhoods and among the lowest-income people, a majority of respondents feel that no one is consistently treated better or worse by the city.

One of the reasons that neighborhood representational anomalies are so well tolerated in these cities is that the vast majority of decisions made by the neighborhood groups affects primarily their neighborhood alone. In Birmingham and

Table 4.2 Perception of Unequal Treatment of Neighborhoods: By Neighborhood Strength

Neighborhood strength index value	Percent agreeing that some groups are always treated better	Percent agreeing that some groups are always treated worse
Low 1	32.9%	36.8%
2	41.5	38.4
3	36.9	36.8
4	41.2	38.7
High 5	36.1	35.0
(N)	(2241)	(2255)
Pearson Chi-Square	8.99 (4 DF)	1.21 (4 DF)

Notes:

Each figure represents the percentage of respondents answering "yes" to the questions detailed below, for respondents living in a neighborhood with an association having the neighborhood strength index value indicated. Neither Chi-Square value is significant at the .05 level.

Full question wording: Thinking about all the types and groups of people and neighborhoods in [city], is there anyone who you think always seems to get treated better than everyone else by the city government?

Is there any type of people, group of people, or neighborhood that you think always seems to get treated worse than everyone else by the city government?

Portland particularly, where the least structural attention is given to balancing population, the larger bodies serve primarily as support systems and advisory channels for the neighborhoods. Citywide decisions are rare, and when they occur, other mechanisms to solicit citizen input are usually employed above and beyond the neighborhood structures. In Dayton, the priority boards with their more equalized representational structure are given more clout than the

Table 4.3 Perception of Unequal Treatment of Neighborhoods: By Neighborhood Socioeconomic Status

Neighborhood socioeconomic category	Percent agreeing that some groups are always treated better	Percent agreeing that some groups are always treated worse
Low	41.7%	43.1%
Moderate	39.8	39.8
High	36.6	33.6
(N)	(2505)	(2524)
Pearson Chi-Square	3.791 (2 DF)	13.633[a] (2 DF)

Notes:

Each figure represents the percentage of respondents answering "yes" to the questions detailed in Table 4.2, for respondents living in a neighborhood in the socioeconomic category indicated (low = index values 1, 2, 3; moderate = index values 4, 5, 6; high = index values 7, 8, 9, 10; see Table 3.7 and Appendix E).

a. Chi-Square value is significant at better than the .01 level.

neighborhoods on many decisions. And St. Paul, the city with relatively equal populations to start with, also has one of the few major citywide decision-making processes: the Capital Improvement Budget Committee, which is drawn entirely from the neighborhoods, initiating all capital project allocations for the city on a biannual basis.[3]

Multi-Issue Responsiveness

> *Within the context of a continuously evolving set of priorities determined by participants, the organization should tackle any and all issues that are brought before it.*

It is clearly not enough to have an equal vote if the issues are so restricted as to be meaningless. The Dahl-derived criterion from Chapter 2 perhaps states the case most completely:

Any citizen who perceives a set of alternatives, at least one of which he or she regards as preferable to any of the alternatives presently scheduled, can insert his or her preferred alternatives among those scheduled for the participation process.

In many ways, this is the same problem discussed by Bachrach and Baratz in their influential analysis of the two faces of power.[4] It is a question of who can put their issues, whatever issues they choose, onto the decision-making agenda.

This criterion for effective representation, unlike the role of equality, is one of the least fulfilled in its application to voting. In a representative democracy, very few alternatives may actually be inserted on the schedule by the voter or even for the voter's consideration. Certainly a variety of candidates can and do run for public office. Yet, except in the rare case of an overriding "hot button" issue, the office typically represents a whole host of major concerns on which voters have a variety of differing opinions. Even though observers such as Nie and Verba have seen a growth in recent decades of the "coherence of political attitudes" among voters,[5] this broad liberal/conservative coherence does not mean that large numbers of individuals hold identical views on each of the issues. In reality, groupings are different for abortion, the death penalty, welfare reform, health care, environmental concerns, and so on. In fact, very few individuals fit an exact ideological profile. Consequently, each candidate by necessity represents a compromise among these issues. It may almost be claimed that only by running as a candidate oneself can an individual realistically insert a separate "alternative" onto the schedule.

Nor, as we have seen, do parties improve this situation substantially. The same kind of compromise vote must be made whether or not strong, responsible parties exist in a two-party system. And when parties fail to offer a clear distinction of ideology and direction, as they have failed to do consistently at least since World War II, they provide even less opportunity to insert an effective alternative onto the schedule than do individual candidates.

Ballot questions do offer one means for individuals (or, more realistically, organizations) to insert their issues onto the decision-making agenda, at least in the twenty-four states and variety of municipalities where this option is available. In some ways this process comes close to Dahl's ideal of citizen agenda-setting. But it also has a number of drawbacks. The initial obstacles are extremely high for a single individual—collecting tens to hundreds of thousands of signatures to put a question on the ballot is no mean task—and the barrier is very poorly related to citizen interest. If you have enough funds to hire the collectors, it is almost as easy to solicit signatures for a very unpopular issue as for a very popular one, as any campaign organization knows. Second, because the exact wording of a measure is fixed before the issue even enters the public arena, the opportunity for a deliberative process, as we discuss in the next section, is severely limited. And third, even though the range of specific issue choices is much greater than it is for a candidate vote, it is much less than occurs in any even marginally participatory organization, forum, advisory committee, or other face-to-face discussion.

Advocacy groups also offer a far greater opportunity to find an alternative close to the one an individual may wish to insert, but they too have significant limitations. First, as we have noted, many points of view have no strong organizational representation. Second, and even more important, many such groups are essentially single-issue groups. If you agree with the fundamental premises of the groups, you join. If you don't, you stay away. There is generally little room in such groups for deliberation outside the realm of priorities within their narrowly defined objectives, unless it is deliberation about strategies and tactics to achieve those objectives. These groups provide an excellent mechanism to shape coherent positions on an issue which then can be presented to the ultimate decision makers—whether they be legislators or the public as a whole. But the groups themselves are poor substitutes for those decision makers.

Open-ended, multi-issue groups like many neighborhood associations, Alinsky-style community groups, citizen-research organizations, and other grassroots groups with a mission to incorporate the views of a heterogeneous community, perform extremely well on this criteria. Their come-one, come-all openness, their face-to-face meetings, their reluctance to limit anyone's opportunity to speak, and above all, their prima-facie insistence on their right to speak out and act on any issue they choose, provide a high degree of assurance that an individual's issue can and will make it onto their agenda—if it has at least a small degree of resonance with others in the organization, and often even if it does not.

The neighborhood groups in this study fit this model well. In Birmingham, Dayton, and Portland, virtually all the neighborhood organizations operated very much as we have just described. And through their representatives to the community-level groups and citywide Citizen Advisory Board in Birmingham, through the district coalition boards in Portland, and through the neighborhood representatives to the priority boards in Dayton (which are in many boards co-equal to the precinct-elected representatives), these neighborhood agendas also make it to the agenda of the city on a regular basis.

The efficacy of this process is significantly dependent, however, upon the strength of the individual neighborhood organizations, as Table 4.4 demonstrates. In neighborhoods where the organizations are strong, participation is channeled through them to a high degree, with more than 23 percent of all respondents involved in them in some way during a two-year period. In neighborhoods where the organizations are weak, however, these organizations capture less than 10 percent of the respondents, while other groups, such as issue

Table 4.4 Type of Participation

	Percent who participate in each type of group					
Neighborhood strength index value	Neighborhood group	Issue group	Crime watch	Service or social group	None	(N)
Low 1	10.1%	9.8%	5.0%	15.7%	59.3%	(337)
2	9.4	11.5	7.6	17.3	54.3	(741)
3	11.9	12.6	4.8	16.2	54.6	(842)
4	18.4	11.1	6.1	15.6	48.9	(642)
High 5	23.4	14.6	7.3	15.1	39.6	(192)

Pearson Chi-Square = 61.46, significant at better than the .01 level.

Exceptions

7	5.3%	13.3%	4.0%	13.3%	64.0	(75)
8	29.9	9.0	7.5	11.9	41.8	(67)

Note:

Each figure represents the percentage of respondents within each neighborhood strength category who participate in the type of organization indicated. Exceptions are treated as missing values for the purposes of the Chi-Square analysis.

advocacy organizations, crime watches, and particularly social and service organizations, remain relatively well-attended. The number of people not involved in any group is dramatically higher.

The "exceptions" in the neighborhood strength classification—neighborhoods where structure and participation fail to match—are dramatic indeed. Those with an index value label of 7 (groups with relatively strong neighborhood organizational structure but poor participation) show remarkably high levels of issue advocacy participation, while the crime-watch and service-group participation, along with the neighborhood group participation, is the lowest of all the categories. Those with an index value label of 8 (groups with relatively weak neighborhood organizational structure but uncharacteristically high neighborhood participation) tend to yield among the highest participation rates for crime-watch groups as well as the neighborhood associations, but are at the lowest levels of participation with other groups.

In spite of their multi-issue strengths, the neighborhood organizations examined in this study have some serious limitations on this criterion. Their issues focus heavily upon either land-use issues or issues that primarily affect only their own neighborhood. Many of the issues we examined fall into six major categories: neighborhood-scale development, city-scale development, environmental concerns, crime prevention, neighborhood-based planning, and neighborhood-level budget initiatives. Rarely would the organizations consider action upon other citywide or big-picture issues such as human services, health care, abortion, unemployment, taxation, or citywide budgets, and almost never even touch upon issues dealt with primarily by state and federal governments. Even the educational system, whose schools were no longer neighborhood schools and whose administration, unlike most other agencies, generally failed to recognize the neighborhood groups as legitimate community representatives, was largely off limits.

The reason for this systematic self-limitation of issues seems largely to reflect a realistic assessment of their power. In each city, the neighborhood associations have been recognized and nurtured primarily by community development or planning agencies that themselves have a major focus in one or more of the six areas described above. This focus remains even though in Portland the Office of Neighborhood Associations is an entirely independent "cabinet-level" agency, and in Dayton the Neighborhood Affairs Office is located formally within the Human Services Department. This nurturing is possible because the political sphere of action for the organizations on these issues—a sphere that does not threaten the broader prerogatives of the mayor and city councillors—is at the neighborhood level. The neighborhood associations have the power to act at the neighborhood level, so it is those issues that are at the core of their agenda.

If neighborhood associations were collectively able to determine issues facing the entire city, the state, or even the nation, there is every reason to believe that their multi-issue focus would expand to match that new ability. The groups have proven their ability to handle any issue that comes along within their neighborhood scope. And the work of other organizations over the last fifteen years—particularly the Kettering Foundation's Domestic Issues Forum and the Connecticut-based Study Circles Resource Center—have shown that small groups of citizens, engaging in forms of face-to-face discussion similar to those in these neighborhood organizations, can successfully tackle some of the most complex national issues, from racism, unemployment, and welfare reform to the federal budget deficit and even foreign policy.[6]

Yet the question remains whether these neighborhood organizations, having a long history of issue limitation for the reasons cited above, could break out of that mold. It will not be easy, because these issues have become an essential part of their self-definition, and are now the reason that people become active in them. One alternative may be to develop parallel neighborhood-based organizations that have all the same characteristics as the traditional ones, with the exception that they are asked from the beginning to deal with the larger issues as part of a citywide, statewide, or even national policy process. More realistically, perhaps, would be the formation of committees within each existing neighborhood group to begin to deal with these larger issues as the opportunity for influence arises. Once accepted, such committees could well become larger and larger parts of the essential nature of these organizations, and allow them to become fully multi-issue organizations in the sense we have discussed.

Internal Democracy

To the maximum extent possible, the activities and operations of such organizations should take place in a democratic, deliberative manner.

Even if an organization is broadly inclusive of all segments of the community and is open to working on all issues that arise, any claim to be the basis for a participatory democracy quickly evaporates if its operations are tightly controlled and manipulated by a small cabal operating in its own vested interests. The internal democracy of the grassroots organization is at the center of our entire discussion. It has two facets, one egalitarian and one deliberative:

The *egalitarian nature of an organization* implies a decision-making process with clearly defined rules and procedures that enable each individual to understand what is going on, how those rules apply, and at what point a final decision will be reached. It is also a process that allows each individual to participate at each stage of the process on an equal footing with all other participants.

The *deliberative nature of an organization* implies an ongoing interaction among participants in an attempt to understand the facts of the case, identify the relevant values at stake, and engage in an extended dialogue, building up a potential solution layer by layer as agreement is reached.[7]

The electoral process, as we have come to know it, is virtually all egalitarianism and no deliberation. It certainly meets the fourth and fifth of Dahl's criteria (described in Chapter 2): that the weight assigned to the choice of each individual is identical, and that the alternative with the greatest number of votes is declared the winning choice. But even this egalitarian aspect is true only in the very limited sense, as applied to voting itself. The political campaign, however, is also a part of the electoral process. And the campaign is understood and controlled by a very few seeking to get a message out to the very many. Access to the campaign is highly restricted by money, social status, and political skills. In this sense, the electoral process has a seriously non-egalitarian strain. But of even greater concern is that its deliberative character is virtually nonexistent for the average voter. For most, the extent of deliberation is five minutes in the voting booth once every year, or two years, or four. The one-way messaging is far from being a deliberative process. It focuses on candidate personality, strategies, and polish, and gives scant attention to the issues that will be determined by the vote. For ballot questions, at least the issues are the focus of the electoral process, but all the other limitations, both egalitarian and deliberative, apply.

Political parties could in theory overcome many of these problems. But history suggests that this is unlikely. The lack of internal democracy in parties; their frequent failure even to come up with a detailed, coherent program; and the rarity of party unity or discipline on issues were all discussed in detail in Chapter 2. In none of the cities of this study, for example, was any party organization an active participant in any of the major issues discussed by administrators or citizen activists—with the possible exception of one or two issues on the agenda of a reform party faction in Birmingham which was attempting to challenge the entrenched Democratic Party machinery there. In fact, in most cases our interview respondents proudly asserted that the issues were dealt with in a "nonpartisan" fashion. The problem seems to be that local party organizations in America today see themselves almost exclusively as agents of an electoral campaign. Whatever happens between elections or on issues outside the electoral process is seen by them, as well as other political actors, as largely outside the party's sphere of action. Consequently, "partisan" activity is literally synonymous with polarization and winner-take-all results—the antithesis of the deliberative process.

So far we have left the representative out of our consideration of the egalitarian and deliberative character of the political process. Yet it can be argued that, in a representative democracy, it is what the representative does between elections that embodies the deliberative ideal. It is true that, leaving aside blatant anti-egalitarian distortions due to status and seniority, the legislative body meets most of the criteria we have set out in this section—for the legislators themselves. But a democracy is not defined solely by the manner in which representatives interact with each other. The other half of the equation is how the representatives interact with their constituents. To evaluate this we return to the discussion that we began in Chapter 2 and drew out further in the first section of the current chapter. We have acknowledged that it is the representative, or rather the collective body of representatives, which takes the action, but have asserted that two other elements of the representative process are critical: the representative assessing the interests of his constituency and using that as a basis for his role in the legislative decision; and the representative being responsive to the individuals within that constituency.

In practice, neither of these elements are significantly deliberative. In assessing the interests of a constituency, the most common systematic approach is to use a public opinion poll. This is inherently a one-way process from interviewee to interviewer, with no interaction whatsoever between constituents and no possibility of working out solutions to a problem. Other forms of interest assessment are either indirect—hearing from a lobby group representative what she asserts the constituent interests are—or haphazard—relying on the intensity of constituent mail or phone calls.

Responsiveness in a typical Congressional district of 500,000 people is even more problematic. No matter how diligent the representative and her/his staff, only a tiny fraction of the constituents can ever talk to, meet with, or receive direct services from the representative. And for most of those that do, the interaction is sporadic, sharply limited in content, and at best involve a discussion exclusive to the representative and individual constituent or group. It almost never involves constituents themselves as equal partners. In much smaller districts, such as a city council ward in a small city, representatives occasionally approach the deliberative ideal much more closely, holding extensive working sessions with constituents on an ongoing basis to deal with specific issues. But even then, such activities are rare and often limited to a typical "public hearing" format consisting mostly of one side speaking and the other listening, with little or no opportunity for constituents to interact among themselves or build solutions.

Neighborhood-style organizations, on the other hand, carry out the deliberative process exceedingly well. Most of those in the cities in this study function with issue committees of no more than fifteen to twenty people, providing an opportunity for all participants to "speak their piece" and work with other participants toward a common solution. In most situations, it is relatively easy for an individual to put her/his own issue on the agenda, and have it considered to the extent that it reflects the interests of others in the group. Discussion continues on a regular basis—usually monthly or twice monthly, enabling alternative approaches to major issues to be considered, reshaped, and put into final form. The potential certainly exists for cliques to grow and unwelcome participants to be shut out of the process, especially since neighborhood leaders are rarely trained facilitators. Yet in all the interviews of this study with administrators, citizen group leaders, neighborhood participants, and survey respondents, charges of exclusionary practices were extremely rare. And, as we saw in the first section of this chapter, the bottom line is that citizens generally trust the associations to be open to their ideas and to represent their interests.

Perhaps the most common concern expressed by politicians and administrators about such organizations is their competency in dealing with complex issues of modern government. It is certainly true that the participants are not usually experts in housing, community development, environmental protection, or any of the myriad issues the organizations commonly handle on a day-to-day basis. But they do have a vision for what they want the community to become, and an awareness of problems affecting their daily lives that need to be addressed. And they tend to consult with the experts whenever the situations demand such expertise. In the cities of this study, the relationship between city agencies and the neighborhood groups generally demanded that such consultation take place. If it had not, the agency officials would direct neighborhood participants to such experts before their next round of discussions. It is significant that while delays, conflict, and some degree of frustration were cited by agency officials as occasional byproducts of the participation process, the problem of neighborhood competency on the issues in which they were involved, or even an overly parochial attitude, were rarely expressed.[8] Instead, we repeatedly heard the comment that "an appropriate balance" was achieved in their city between neighborhood concerns and the broader citywide viewpoint addressed by city councillors and city officials.

Openness

To the maximum extent possible, the organizations should be continuously open and responsive to new participants.

Michels's "iron law of oligarchy," mentioned earlier, applies to the neighborhood organization as well as it does to massive federal bureaucracies. Oligarchy to an democratic organization is like death to an individual organism: sooner or later it happens, and it ends all democratic functioning. Yet, like successful organisms, new democratic life can continuously refresh the organization and keep it alive, energetic, and responsive.

For citizen organizations, the key to this renewal is a continuous supply of new members and the new ideas they bring. When an organization wraps protective barriers around itself and excludes new participation and different approaches, it ossifies, becomes oligarchic, and generally loses its political impact. When it works to attract new members, encourages their active participation, and expands its repertoire to include their interests, the encroaching oligarchy is pushed back or chipped away.

Among citizen groups, neighborhood associations are particularly vulnerable to this process of ossification. With small, fixed boundaries and a regular constituency, it is a perennial problem for such groups to identify people within their area to assume leadership roles and devote the necessary energy to keeping the organization alive and active. In fact, one of the most serious complaints we saw from critics of the neighborhood associations within the cities of this study was that, to paraphrase, "the same leaders have run that organization since it started . . . they exclude others who disagree with them and prevent the group from addressing the real needs of the neighborhood." While this perspective was expressed in fewer than a half dozen of the more than four hundred in-depth interviews our research team conducted, it was consistent enough to warrant further investigation. Where the team could examine historical records of neighborhood leadership, we found that for most organizations, leadership changed on a regular basis, usually every three or four years or more often, but that for a small number, perhaps as many as 10 percent of the organizations, essentially the same leadership positions had been filled by the same individuals since the groups began, between ten and fifteen years earlier.

We also found that at least two major mechanisms helped to keep the organizations open and accountable. The first was the pressure from outside organizations, corporations, or agencies who were not always supportive of the positions of the neighborhood association. The second was the pressure from city officials, who, in recognizing the group as the formal representative of that neighborhood, required certain proofs of openness and demonstrations of accountability on a continuous basis.

A clear example of the first mechanism occurred in one Portland neighborhood which became concerned over a huge new "suburban-style" shopping center in their area, to be developed by the city's largest retailer. Before the controversy began, they were a fairly small organization, with perhaps twenty or thirty people attending their regular meetings. But as they began to voice opposition to certain features of the proposed center, the developers commissioned a poll of people in the neighborhood that they said showed a majority in favor of the shopping complex (although the actual survey questions and methodology were never made public). As a consequence, the organization launched a major counteroffensive, canvassed the entire neighborhood, and attracted more than four hundred people to their next series of meetings on the issue. And in response to internal criticism, they began to include full majority and minority positions in all reports of their meetings. Eventually the shopping center was built, but with elaborate landscaping and traffic controls that substantially ameliorated the effects on the neighborhood that had concerned the organization.

The second mechanism, that of pressure from the city officials, was visible in each of the cities we looked at. One form it took in each city was the insistence on, and financial support for, notification of every resident in the neighborhood about the group's activities. We will look at these activities in more detail in Chapter 5, on organizational outreach. In general, the city's concerns were predicated on their need to protect their political backside. By recognizing the neighborhood organizations as spokespersons for their community, city agencies rely on them to do this job credibly. If they depend on the viewpoints that the neighborhoods express to accurately reflect sentiment in the neighborhood, and this later proves, through the emergence of a strong political opposition, to be false, the agencies and the elected officials behind them can be in serious trouble. A revealing expression of this dynamic is provided in Portland by the development of a thirteen-page set of "Guidelines for Neighborhood Associations, District Coalition Boards, and the Office of Neighborhood Associations" worked out over an eighteen-month period by representatives of the neighborhoods and the city. It describes requirements for nondiscrimination, open meetings, public records, nonprofit corporation status (for the coalition boards), and a number of other rights and responsibilities of the neighborhoods and the boards as representatives of their community. The guidelines were formally incorporated by city ordinance with the finding that "certain minimum standards for neighborhood associations and district coalition boards are necessary so that those groups can be recognized as an important and bona fide communicative link between the city and its citizens."[9]

As a result of this careful effort to maintain openness, our research team found that respondents to the public opinion poll generally believe that the neighborhood associations were open to their participation. As part of a series of questions about what the respondent would do in reaction to a proposal to "change city services or to change your community in a way you and your neighbors disapprove of," we specifically inquired about their expectation of being offered the opportunity to participate in the neighborhood association process. The results are shown in Table 4.5. In all neighborhood strength categories and for all respondent SES levels, at least 53 percent of the respondents felt that the opportunity for participation would be provided. This rose to more than 78 percent for the highest SES respondents in the strongest neighborhoods. Similar results were obtained, as shown in Table 4.6, in the follow-up question asking if they would actually become involved with the neighborhood association in such a case. The range in of positive response to this question was from 49 percent to over 73 percent.

These tables also reveal a very important characteristic of the stronger neighborhood organizations: variation with income is significantly reduced. For neighborhoods on the lower end of the neighborhood strength scale, the differences between high SES and low SES respondents is always significant

Table 4.5 Expected Offer of Involvement Opportunity

Neighborhood strength index value	Percent believing they would be offered opportunity				
	Low SES	Moderate SES	High SES	(N)	Chi-Square
Low 1	53.7%	63.0%	73.3%	(323)	7.66[a]
2	53.0	65.1	74.3	(654)	17.59[b]
3	61.6	69.5	78.8	(747)	13.40[b]
4	55.0	68.7	76.6	(587)	20.15[b]
High 5	63.8	66.7	78.3	(182)	3.46

Notes:
Each figure represents the percentage of respondents answering "yes" to the question below, for respondents living in a neighborhood with an association having the neighborhood strength index value indicated. Socioeconomic status is measured here on an individual level.

a. Significant at the .05 level or beyond.

b. Significant at the .01 level or beyond.

Full question wording: Let's say that your local neighborhood association was going to address this [major neighborhood] issue at its next meeting. Do you think you would be offered the opportunity to become involved in the neighborhood association process?

Table 4.6 Acceptance of Involvement Opportunity

Neighborhood strength index value	Percent reporting they would become involved				
	Low SES	Moderate SES	High SES	(N)	Chi-Square
Low 1	49.1%	58.1%	70.8%	(312)	8.58[a]
2	53.1	71.2	66.3	(632)	19.18[b]
3	57.6	63.8	73.5	(722)	10.10[b]
4	61.8	61.2	58.2	(566)	0.54
High 5	61.4	53.1	68.2	(174)	3.10

Notes:
Each figure represents the percentage of respondents answering yes to the question below, for respondents living in a neighborhood with an association having the neighborhood strength index value indicated. Socioeconomic status is measured here on an individual level.

a. Significant at the .05 level or beyond.

b. Significant at the .01 level or beyond.

Full question wording: If the neighborhood association did offer you the opportunity to be involved when it addressed such an issue, do you think you would actually get involved?

(at the .05 level or better), yielding a gap in some cases of more than 20 percent. For neighborhoods in the highest strength category in Table 4.5 and the highest two categories in Table 4.6, however, these differences are no longer statistically significant, in one case yielding a gap between high and low SES respondents as low as 3.6 percent. The ever-present tendency for high-income people to participate more than low-income people in political action of all types is not eliminated by strong neighborhood associations, but it does seem to be significantly moderated.

Network Maintenance

> *The group should have a strong, ongoing relationship with a support network that can help it to maintain these characteristics over time.*

Ensuring that all segments of the community continuously have the opportunity to be involved in open, multi-issue, egalitarian, deliberative bodies is no small task. It requires a level of resources and commitment that can seldom be attained in purely voluntary organizations. Even in cities where strong neighborhood groups are a tradition, the active organizations that exist at any one time typically cover neighborhoods that contain only a fraction of the city's population. As with other types of grassroots citizen groups, a lifespan of more than five or six years is the exception.

The ability to maintain the network and keep it available to all citizens is thus a major component of the participation organizations in each of the cities of this study. It involves at least five major elements:

First, a citywide organization or agency that has a commitment to network maintenance as a major part of its mission is needed. In each of the four cities, this organization was a separate bureau or agency staffed by the city itself (although in St. Paul and Birmingham the central neighborhood participation staff was housed respectively within the city's Planning and Economic Development and Community Development departments). This kind of agency, within city government, is typical of most communities that are able to maintain such networks. Only in a few American cities, such as Baltimore, have completely independent neighborhood coalitions been able to function in a similar a similar citywide role.

Second, such a citywide organization needs full-time staff who can help new neighborhood associations develop and existing neighborhoods solve basic structural problems. In the four cities, this central staff ranges from more than a dozen in Birmingham to a single person in St. Paul (who, we understand, has now been phased out—but other staff within the Planning and Economic Development Department are serving a similar supportive role for the neighborhoods there).

Third, there is a need for sufficient ongoing financial support for individual neighborhoods or neighborhood coalitions to allow basic organizational services to be maintained, at a minimum to provide for neighborhood-based staff (even if only part-time) and regular communication to all neighborhood residents. As we saw in Table 3.1, the support from the city itself in the four cities ranged in 1987 from a little less than $500,000 to more than $1.2 million (including central staff; but excluding all development and capital funds that also were controlled in whole or part by the neighborhood groups). In these cities, the basic funds come from general city revenues and federal block grants, but other funding mechanisms are certainly possible, including some form of membership dues (presumably by ability to pay) or even some form of tax check-off.

Fourth, neighborhood offices and community centers must exist for individual neighborhoods or coalitions. The necessary work goes beyond that which can be done entirely out of volunteers' homes and church basements. In St. Paul, with its larger neighborhood boundaries, each of its District Councils has its own office, often housed in a community center containing large meeting spaces, recreational facilities, and offices for other community organizations. In Portland and Dayton the coalitions each have several staff to support their constituent neighborhood associations, most of whom are all-volunteer. Only in Birmingham do the support staff all work out of offices in City Hall, a situation unique to the somewhat more paternalistic system that grew out of the rise of the city's African-Americans, as part of the neighborhood system, to their first real political power in the city.

Fifth, structural, contractual, and political arrangements must be made to ensure that the neighborhoods themselves retain ownership and control of a substantial part of the participatory network, despite substantial levels of city funding. In Birmingham, this has included election of neighborhood officers at the polls and allocation of capital improvement funds, by formula, to each neighborhood group. In Portland and Dayton this has included coalition boards made up entirely of representatives from the neighborhood groups or representatives elected by precinct. Portland has also developed a system by which these independent boards contract with the city to provide "citizen participation services." In St. Paul, each neighborhood has its own bylaws and many are separately incorporated, some raising the majority of their own funding from local and foundation donors.

Each of the five propositions made in this chapter has been shown to be an essential ingredient in the core structure of any participatory democracy. The neighborhood associations in the cities of this study have many of the characteristics required by these propositions, particularly in their ability to offer direct involvement in a broadly based deliberative process to all segments of the community. But they are also substantially deficient in some areas, such as the range of issues they currently address, and their dependence upon the support of some of the same government bodies they seek to oversee. Starting from this core, we now need to look in two directions: out to the people and the communities they seek to involve; and up to the issues, policies, and governments they aspire to manage.

Chapter 5

Aggressive Outreach

Democracy is of little value if kept secret. Many organizations can have a highly democratic core and egalitarian, deliberative internal processes, but if they fail in relating to the rest of the community, they fail as a participatory democracy. If the typical community member has no opportunity to be actively involved, if he/she is unaware of that opportunity, or if he/she is not even aware that the so-called participatory organization exists, how can the organization in any sense represent that individual?

Of Dahl's conditions for democracy considered in Chapter 2, the first three hinge on this point. That is: (1) there is no way in which individuals can insert an alternative on the decision-making agenda if they do not know that an agenda is being formed or if they are excluded from the formation process; (2) individuals certainly do not possess identical information about the alternatives if they are not even aware the alternatives exist or have information about how to find them; (3) individuals cannot participate in the decision-making process if a realistic opportunity to participate is not provided for them.

The problem is twofold. First, providing a realistic opportunity for all members of a community to participate takes substantial resources. These are resources that community leaders may not have, or may not be willing to expend for this purpose (especially since an effective outreach effort may be seen as diminishing their own personal influence). This is often compounded by the lack of realization of how much effort is really needed to accomplish the task. Second, citizens have a lot of other things on their minds. For most people, most of the time, politics and government is a minor blip on the radar screen, drowned out by personal, family, and economic pressures and concerns. The responsibility of voting every few years is considered to be some sort of civic duty by many; the responsibility of participating beyond voting is rarely so considered.

Political parties know what outreach is all about—when the election campaign comes around. But they almost never see their role as stimulating participation between elections. Outreach efforts such as door-to-door canvassing, massive phone-call campaigns, saturation mailings, literature drops, or media ads are undertaken by parties between elections at a tiny fraction of the scale they attain during the last few months of an election campaign. This is true even when the issues most central to the party platform are on the verge of being decided by a legislature or agency proceeding. Parties simply are not in the business of non-electoral participation.

Most advocacy groups, on the other hand, are at the peak of their outreach performance between elections. Some, such as those that focus on lobbying, engage in most of the same tactics as electoral campaigns, but generally with far fewer resources. Others, such as those that tackle specific community issues involving, for example, a nearby hazardous waste site or a recent rash of muggings, may actually far surpass the intensity of election campaigns, especially in terms of door-to-door canvassing and other forms of personal contact. But such efforts are almost always contained in a very small geographic area— often a matter of a few square blocks.

All of the outreach efforts we have considered so far, however, differ in one fundamental respect from those required of a participation organization: they seek to recruit people into an effort to support a predefined position or candidate, while the participation organization must engage people in an open-ended effort to work on problems that may not have an obvious or immediate solution. The issue and candidate campaigns may have an easy appeal, as when an imminent threat has already alarmed the neighborhood, or a much more difficult task, as when a candidate has accumulated strong negatives in the region. Either way, they can draw stark contrasts, raise as many red flags as possible about the "other side," and promise nirvana. The participation organization, on the other hand, is primarily selling a process, a community venture. Since it is attempting to bring all sides in the community together on an issue, it cannot generally afford to single out one side of a conflict as the enemy. This can, but need not, lead to a very low-key, unexciting campaign where the issues at stake never become clear.

Since at least the days of Saul Alinsky's Back of the Yards organizing efforts in Chicago, however, the elements of outreach campaigns that can be both energizing and participatory have been demonstrated.[1] Alinsky's organizations, and literally hundreds of others that have followed his model through the Industrial Areas Foundation, National People's Action, the Association of Community Organizations for Reform Now (ACORN), the Pacific Institute for

Community Organization (PICO), Citizen Action, and other training and community organizing networks have demonstrated the power of this approach.[2] Gary Delgado, in reviewing the community organizing movement and particularly the role of ACORN in it, describes the model ACORN uses for its six- to eight-week drives to start up a new community group.[3] He identifies seven stages: research and analysis, initial contact work, developing an organizing committee and campaign issue, preparing for a neighborhood meeting, holding the meeting, initiating "collective social action," and finally, evaluation of the results. The role of the organizer during the first phase of contact work is particularly important in illustrating the scope of outreach activity that is required by this model:

In this phase an organizer puts together a list of contacts from either a voter registration list, a criss-cross directory or even a "safe petition." . . . A list of "hot contacts" is not simply material for a mass mailing; it is an invaluable resource that may be transformed into the lifeblood of the organization—its members. Functionally, contact development trains the organizer in a number of skills: it develops a set of work standards (the model demands between twenty and forty contacts per day during the drive); it tests the organizer's ability to be systematic (each contact is spoken with twice and receives two letters and a phone call, all in the space of six weeks); and finally, contact work supports the organization through dues (45 percent of ACORN's budget is supplied by membership dues, and almost 70 percent of that is collected not through the mail, but by direct contact with members in meetings and during doorknocking).[4]

This outreach intensity generates results. Using these kind of techniques, groups such as COPS (Communities Organized for Public Service) are able to bring together as many as 8,000 people from the lowest income neighborhoods in San Antonio to a single event, and make extremely effective use of "people power." In fact, during the 1980s, they were probably the strongest single community group in the country.[5] Such efforts are particularly important when attempting to bring in more low income people to the participation process. As many studies have demonstrated, and we confirmed in *The Rebirth of Urban Democracy,* a strong tendency exists in all forms of political activity for people of low socioeconomic status to participate substantially less than people of higher socioeconomic status.[6] To achieve a balance of interests from the entire community, any participatory organization needs to recognize this tendency and counter it with even more intensive outreach efforts in its lowest income areas. The type of organizing conducted by ACORN and other similar groups is critical for meeting these goals.

The neighborhood groups in this study conduct some of this kind of organizing, some of the time, but do not meet the very high levels that ACORN and other Alinsky-style groups achieve most of the time. The neighborhood advantage in the cities of this study is that they are able to reach and involve people on an equal footing from all parts of the city. Their disadvantage is that they are spread too thin to be as successful in mobilizing people as the Alinsky organizations.

Nevertheless, the overall result of the outreach activities in these cities is quite impressive, especially in those areas with the strongest neighborhood groups, as Table 5.1 demonstrates. In the highest neighborhood strength category, more than 45 percent of the respondents who were asked a question about contacts reported that they had been personally contacted to take part in neighborhood association activities during the last two years (only respondents who previously indicated that they had "heard of the system of neighborhood associations" in their city were asked this question, about 59 percent of the total sample). For the lowest neighborhood strength category, the number falls to less than half the peak, but is still a respectable 19.4 percent. As we saw before, the neighborhoods with exceptionally low and high participation for their level of structure (index values 7 and 8, respectively), again fall into the extremes of the response, respectively falling several percentage points below or above the indicated contact rates for any of the standard neighborhood strength categories.

The basic outreach efforts in these cities accomplish several additional objectives to varying degrees, including development of interpersonal relationships, providing timely information to and responses from community members, maintaining a level of preparedness to deal with sudden crises in the

Table 5.1 Contact by Neighborhood Association

Neighborhood strength index value	Yes	No or not sure	(N)
Low 1	19.4%	80.6%	(144)
2	27.4	72.6	(369)
3	26.7	73.3	(423)
4	31.8	68.2	(377)
High 5	45.9	54.1	(111)

Pearson Chi-Square = 24.88, significant at better than the .01 level.

Exceptions			
7	16.7%	83.3%	(42)
8	54.5	45.5	(33)

Note:
Full question wording: In the past two years, has anyone personally contacted you to ask you to take part in neighborhood association activities? (Asked of respondents who had heard of the system of neighborhood associations in the city).

community, and reaching the hardest to reach within the community. We will briefly examine each of these accomplishments in turn.

Interpersonal Relationships

A structure of involvement is needed that enables the development of an extensive set of interpersonal relationships.

This structure includes at least three elements. First, as we saw in Chapter 4, the basic organizational units are open, accessible, and democratic. But more than that, they are relatively low-key settings that tend to foster the development of friendships and understanding even among those who initially disagree on many issues. Typical meetings involve a few dozen people sitting around a table discussing their concerns with agency staff, candidates, developers, or just among themselves, with the understood goal of trying to reach an acceptable agreement for all concerned. Of course, each group has its own independent personality, and like any decision-making body, some groups at some times generate a great deal of heat with little light. But most groups seem to work in a constructive mode most of the time. And there are many forms of involvement and leadership roles, from researcher to advocate and organizer to project volunteer, that allow those with different skills and interests to take active parts.

Second, while nearly all the neighborhood organizations are heavily volunteer-dependent, all have the support of at least a skeleton staff structure. As we saw in Table 3.1, each of the cities of this study except Birmingham has a total of twenty-eight staff or more (full-time equivalent) whose primary mission is to keep the neighborhood organizations open and active and to facilitate volunteers' neighborhood and city-hall activities. Most of these work out of the neighborhood offices. They don't often engage in ACORN-style community organizing activities (a few do), but they do a great deal to maintain the organizational fabric, the nitty-gritty day-to-day work that enables the neighborhoods and their coalitions to survive. And they ensure full-time accessibility of the neighborhood group to anybody who stops by. In fact, as our research team concluded in a review of the entire project, "If only one piece of information were used to rate the strength of a citywide participation effort, the most useful measure would be the number of full-time staff devoted to citizen and neighborhood support."[7]

Third, nearly all of the organizations have subgroups who help divide up responsibility and bring their activities closer to individual interests. While many of these are working committees of the neighborhood association, some of the larger organizations, especially in St. Paul, incorporate a host of block clubs as part of their basic organizational structure. One St. Paul neighborhood boasts 350 of them. The block clubs help the group stimulate leadership at the most grassroots level possible, and serve basic roles in crime watches and in notifying residents about issues and meetings. The block clubs take extra staff and funding to maintain, but where they exist, they represent a major form of ongoing outreach.

Timely Information

The outreach process must provide timely information to all community members about the issues at stake, and the opportunity to be involved.

The most basic requirement for effective outreach is that people throughout the community receive enough information to allow them to make reasonable decisions about their own roles in the process. This information needs to be frequent, visible, and interesting enough to be heard among the barrage of media and personal demands the average person faces each day. Beyond the personal contact outlined in the section above, most of this occurs in written form in the cities in this study. Some groups also use cable television or the internet to their advantage, but these approaches are still in embryonic form.

Each of the four cities has some form of notification that goes to the local organizations about all city activities that affect their neighborhoods. The neighborhood organizations, in turn, filter this information and pick out the priority issues to communicate to residents on a regular basis. Most groups do some kind of door-to-door distribution of flyers in blocks most affected by a specific issue; for some this happens on an almost weekly basis. In St. Paul, at least one-third of the districts mail to all households in the neighborhood at least quarterly. This is part of the city's Early Notification System (originally termed the "Early Warning System") in which a wide range of specifically designated agency activities is required to be reported to the public according to a timetable spelled out by ordinance.

Most of the broad-based communication, however, occurs through some form of neighborhood newsletter or community newspaper. In Birmingham, it is through neighborhood information packets written by the associations and support staff and mailed out once a month to every household in the city. In Portland, the city contracts with each district coalition to provide enough support to cover all printing and mailing costs to each household at least once a year (and many neighborhoods use donated resources to spread the basic support out for several newsletters a year to all households). In Dayton, the neighborhood process is less regular, but also supported at the coalition (priority board) level. In St. Paul, twelve of the seventeen neighborhoods have full-scale neighborhood newspapers published monthly, bimonthly, or even biweekly. Most are distributed to every household. Some are run by independent citizen groups with a great deal of volunteer labor, while others are run by the District Council itself. In all the cities, these regular publications include activist profiles, a calendar of events, and articles on the hot issues of the month. They serve as a basic link to ensure that every resident is aware of opportunities for them to have a role in the decision-making process.

The cities have also had citywide neighborhood-oriented publications distributed door-to-door, but these have not been as consistently maintained as the neighborhood publications. For several years, Birmingham had a four-page publication called *Cross Town,* focusing on ongoing city programs and the participation system; Dayton has had both Priority Board newsletters and a citywide publication, *Update,* providing similar kinds of information; four of Portland's seven coalitions have newsletters of their own that reach most district households, and the citywide Office of Neighborhood Associations produces a four-page newsletter covering recent success stories ten times a year, sent to all neighborhood officers and anyone else who requests to receive it.

Information Flow from the Community

> *The outreach process must ensure a constant flow of perceptions, concerns, and reactions from community members to the participation groups and citywide decision makers.*

The information flow must be just as effective back from citizens as it is out to them. The in-depth communication, of course, occurs within the face-to-face deliberations we discussed in Chapter 4. But it is important that this communication be supplemented with a much broader scope of feedback that can include those unable to take an active role in the day-to-day activities of the participation groups. Each of the four cities has seen this as a vital activity and implemented some form of broader input.

The most common form of this input is the public opinion survey. Birmingham has used surveys primarily in conjunction with a detailed planning process in about one-quarter of its neighborhoods. Portland conducts a annual citywide survey, highlighting a different feature of city services each year, and Dayton does the same, along with individual surveys conducted by neighborhoods or priority boards, usually in response to a specific issue or proposal. An important feature of Dayton's survey process is its integration into the city's Management by Objectives process. In some cases, specific management objectives are stated in terms of citizen response to this survey (for example, objective: improve citizen satisfaction with park maintenance by 3 percent in 1986; result: objective not obtained, satisfaction remained the same). A summary of these results, along with related performance reports, is included in the city's budget document each year.

In addition to the survey process, Portland and Dayton have a regular Neighborhood Needs reporting system that is part of major agency planning and budget processes. Each neighborhood is asked to identify the most pressing needs it has during the coming year, and to submit specific proposals to the city. A few neighborhoods even do an annual questionnaire to their mailing lists soliciting input for these needs reports. In each city, the coalition offices collect these requests from individual residents, neighborhood groups, and other citizen groups, and distribute them to the appropriate city agencies. They then monitor the agency response and ensure that each requesting party receives an answer directly from that agency—yes, no, or "maybe, if . . . "

Crisis Preparedness

Additional mechanisms to fold in the involvement of much larger numbers than usual are needed when controversies arise and the public interest peaks.

Crises always attract far more participants than the day-to-day routine or long-range planning issues. As we noted earlier, the neighborhood associations in this study are often better than other citizen groups at managing the routine and long-range, but are often not as good as these groups at dealing with crisis. But an effective participatory democracy must be good at both. The long-range issues are a vital part of making the community work: if citizens are not involved, city officials will be the only players in the game. Yet crises also happen, and when they do, they require an effective response involving large numbers of citizens.

Most of the neighborhoods in this study deal with crisis issues on an ad-hoc basis. There are few if any contingency plans or standard modus operandi. This is in substantial contrast to typical Alinsky-style groups, who essentially incorporate the crisis issue into their basic operating framework—practically the only issues they work on become crises at their own instigation. A clear example of this difference involved the sewer extension project in Portland. The city was undergoing a massive annexation program during the time we were there, a project that eventually was to add nearly 100,000 people to the city's residents. As county "unincorporated area" residents, they had become accustomed to septic tanks on their own property. As city residents, under new environmental laws, a sewer system was a must, costing several thousand dollars for every homeowner. Citizens were outraged. The neighborhood groups (which, to be fair, were just gaining a foothold in the new city territory) puttered around with this issue, but were unable to make much progress. But an independent group, the Portland Organizing Project (POP), quickly took up the slack and organized meetings with hundreds of people to protest the sewer costs and procedures. The question is still out on how effective they were at resolving the issues, but POP clearly had taken on the leadership role.

The neighborhood associations need to take a page from community organizing on these types of issues. Alternate operating procedures need to be clearly spelled out and ready to go, with specific agreements to allow shifting of neighborhood and coalition staff assignments as appropriate to meet citizens' concerns when an emergency arises.

Broadening the Base

Ongoing efforts to broaden the base of participation among the lowest-income members of the community are crucial to prevent the exclusion of their interests by default.

As we noted above, participation does not come to all citizens equally easily. Low income people and people with little formal education often are uncomfortable in political settings or when public speaking is required. Personal and economic pressures often keep their focus away from community issues. The bottom line is that if outreach is conducted equally in all parts of a community, rich and poor alike, people of low socioeconomic status will not be represented equally.

In the larger study, our research team found that this concern also extends to minority ethnic and racial populations where they are not large or concentrated enough to have neighborhoods where they predominate.[8] In each of the cities, for example, the black population was large enough to be represented by a number of separate neighborhood associations, and concerns specific to that population seemed to be addressed fairly well. Other populations, such as the American Indians and Laotian Hmong population in St. Paul, and the Vietnamese population in Portland, were thinly scattered across many neighborhoods, and issues of concern to them rarely surfaced on the neighborhood agenda.

The neighborhoods in this study seem to recognize this problem, and occasionally embark on efforts specifically designed to recruit neglected minorities and low-income people into the process. But their efforts do not match the scale of the problem. Participation rates continue to be much lower in minority areas than among the population as a whole. Additional resources need to be shifted into these areas, and the same kind of activities the neighborhood associations conduct so well in general need to be intensified when attempting to reach populations at risk of being excluded. This is another area where the associations can learn from groups like ACORN, which was formed originally to organize welfare recipients and retains many of the perspectives needed to effectively energize low-income people.

Participate Where?

Up to this point in our consideration of outreach, we have seen that the Alinsky-style community organizations have a number of advantages over the neighborhood associations we observed. The intensity of their work enables them to more fully meet a key condition of a participatory democracy—offering a realistic opportunity for all members of the community to participate—than do the activities of the neighborhood associations. But the neighborhood associations have two advantages of their own. The first, as we have already noted, is that the neighborhood associations cover the entire city in the communities we observed. Alinsky-style organizations, in nearly every community where they work, are effective in only a few carefully selected neighborhoods. Second, the clear mission of most Alinsky-style organizations is to attract only certain types of people—low-income people, minorities, or people with very pointed issue concerns. In fact, one of their visible strengths is that they can successfully foster a powerful "we" vs. "they" dynamic that energizes their constituents. COPS is a case in point. Widely cited as one of the best examples of an Alinsky-style group in the country, it has organized only about 30 percent of the population of the city.[9] Parallel organizations that exist in the anglo and black portions of the city are designed to remedy this situation, but are in reality pale shadows of the Hispanic base of COPS. (This is not to detract from the fact that COPS has taken a Hispanic population and Hispanic neighborhoods that were almost totally neglected by city officials and city development projects and made them the most powerful political force in the city.)

Independent advocacy organizations were active and often effective in each of the four cities of our study. In Portland and St. Paul, in fact, Alinsky-style organizations were going head to head with the neighborhood associations (the Portland Organizing Project in the former, and ACORN and Minnesota COACT in the latter). Yet we have already seen one important indication that the impact of the neighborhood associations overshadows that of the advocacy groups in these cities. Going back to Table 4.4, we saw that the total participation in "Issue Groups"—a category that includes all organizations, except the neighborhood groups, that work to influence the results of issues before city government—is comparable to or substantially less than participation in the neighborhood groups at every level of the neighborhood strength index. That is, *participation in the neighborhood groups is greater than that in all other issue groups combined!*[10]

We can explore the impact of neighborhood organizing further by examining the types of activities in which citizens in the neighborhood engage as the neighborhood becomes better and better organized. During the course of the work on *The Rebirth of Urban Democracy,* our research team developed an Index of Community Participation that used the answers to several of our survey questions relating to citizen group participation, working with others to solve a community problem, and helping to form an organization.[11] Table 5.2 shows where individuals fall on this scale as a function of the neighborhood strength index. The relationship is highly significant, yielding a chi-square value of over 50. It is clear from this table that as neighborhood association strength increases, the proportion of both inactive residents and residents active only in "other ways" (crime watches, electoral campaigns, contacting officials, and so on) is reduced dramatically—for inactives from 33.2 percent to 19.0 percent; and for "other" from 23.9 percent to 14.9 percent. Correspondingly, participation in a neighborhood or citizen group at all levels of activity—less than once a month, once a month, and more than once a month—increases substantially. In fact, the once-a-month activity nearly triples from the low to the high end of the neighborhood strength scale. Clearly, effective neighborhood groups do not just shift people from one kind of group to another, but actually move people into higher levels of activity than they would otherwise undertake.

Table 5.2 Level of Participation by Neighborhood Strength

	Index of community participation						
	0	1	2	3	4	5	
				Participated	Participated	Participated	
Neighborhood		Active in	Worked	less than	once a	more than	
strength index	Inactive	other ways	with others	once a month	month	once a month	(N)
Low 1	27.7%	23.9%	28.6%	10.6%	3.8%	5.3%	(339)
2	33.2	19.3	26.9	10.5	4.8	5.3	(751)
3	31.4	22.0	22.4	12.0	6.6	5.6	(851)
4	27.0	20.3	23.6	13.6	9.6	6.0	(649)
High 5	19.0	14.9	28.7	17.4	10.8	9.2	(195)

Pearson Chi-Square = 59.50, significant at better than the .01 level.

Exceptions

7	33.3%	24.4%	24.4%	3.8%	6.4%	7.7%	(78)
8	26.9	10.4	23.9	19.4	6.0	13.4	(67)

Note:
Each figure represents the percentage of respondents in each neighborhood strength category who have participated in at least the indicated activities on the index of community participation. See text for further description of this index.

Table 5.3 Level of Participation by Neighborhood Socioeconomic Status

	Index of community participation						
	0	1	2	3	4	5	
Neighborhood				Participated	Participated	Participated	
socioeconomic		Active in	Worked	less than	once a	more than	
category	Inactive	other ways	with others	once a month	month	once a month	(N)
Low 1	33.7%	20.3%	25.9%	7.2%	6.9%	6.0%	(433)
2	30.7	21.0	26.8	10.7	5.4	5.5	(1398)
High 3	27.5	20.2	22.7	14.8	7.8	7.1	(1288)

Pearson Chi-Square = 37.10, significant at better than the .01 level.

Notes:
Each figure represents the percentage of respondents in each neighborhood socioeconomic category who have participated in at least the indicated activities on the index of community participation (see text discussing Table 5.2 for further description of this index). The neighborhood socioeconomic categories are derived from the neighborhood socioeconomic index (see Table 3.7 and Appendix E) with low = index values 1, 2, 3; moderate = index values 4, 5, 6; high = index values 7, 8, 9, 10.

Correlation of index of community participation with neighborhood strength index:
Correlation coefficient = .095, significant at better than the .01 level.

Partial correlation coefficient, controlling for individual SES and neighborhood economic index value = .0810, significant at better than the .01 level.

This activity also proves to be significantly dependent upon both individual socioeconomic status and neighborhood demographics. As Table 5.3 demonstrates, the relationship is similar to that between activity and strengthened neighborhood associations. The shifts are particularly prominent in terms of a reduction of inactivity and an increase in respondents active in the "less than once a month" category. The overall shifts are significant at better than the .01 level. But the increases in participation once a month or more is far less dramatic as a function of these neighborhood demographics than we saw with neighborhood association strength. Instead of tripling, participation in this category ranges only from 5.5 percent to 7.1 percent of the population.

The overall correlation between the index of community participation and the index of neighborhood strength, shown at the bottom of Table 5.3, is .095, and the partial correlation after controlling for individual SES and for neighborhood socioeconomic status remains strong at .0810. Both correlations are significant at better than the .01 level.

Participate: Why?

To help us better understand what can be done at the community level to make outreach as effective as possible, we can delve into the reasons survey respondents gave for their own participation, or lack of it. Every respondent who was a participant in the neighborhood associations was presented with a list of ten possible reasons[12] in answer to this question:

People take part in organizational activities for different reasons. Please tell me "yes" or "no" for the following whether each reward might be enough reason to increase your work with the neighborhood association by at least two hours per month.

For respondents who were not participants in the neighborhood groups, we replaced the last part of the question with "enough reason to work with the neighborhood association for a least two hours per month." In a similar vein, we presented participants with a list of six possible reasons in answer to the question:

Now I'm going to read a list of things that might keep people from participating in neighborhood associations. Each time I read one please tell me if it is one of the things that might discourage you from continuing to participate in neighborhood association activities.

Again, for respondents who were not participants in the neighborhood groups, we replaced the last part of the question with: "one of the things that has discouraged you from participating in neighborhood association activities."

Table 5.4 shows the overall results for both participants and nonparticipants. The reasons are ordered not as they were asked but by the frequency of a positive response from current participants. The first clear finding is that the rank ordering of results is virtually identical for participants and nonparticipants. Only reasons 1 and 2 were interchanged, as were reasons 3 and 4. It is apparent that participants and nonparticipants have very similar attitudes toward the participation process.

In looking at the individual reasons that people participate, the most important group clearly involves concrete, tangible community benefits: the "solution of a specific problem" and the "provision of a useful service," each receiving over 90 percent "yes" in participant responses. These were also the responses that differed the most from those of nonparticipants, the latter valuing them less highly.

The second group of responses in this same table, with between roughly 65 percent and 75 percent "yes" answers, consists of four reasons that present a more nebulous but still community-oriented or social value: a "sense of contribution," "increased knowledge of the community," "friendship with participants," and an "increased sense of responsibility." The remaining reasons for participating, all of which received less than a 46 percent positive response, tended to reflect more individual benefits: "enhanced professional goals," "material benefits," "political influence," and "prestige."

Looking at the reasons for nonparticipation in the same table, three items separate themselves from the rest of the pack, each with over 50 percent agreement from current participants: the "amount of time it takes," the need to "give up personal matters," and "frustration from a lack of progress." The first two support the hypothesis that the main barrier to overcome in the outreach process is to make participation an attractive alternative for a person's time compared to all other activities he is doing. The fact that "fears of conflict," "need to participate in meetings," and "energy and effort involved" ranked much lower as reasons to avoid involvement, suggest that the barriers to participation that stem from intimidation with the process, at least in these communities, are not significant problems.

One of the most interesting comparisons between participants and nonparticipants is the large difference between these respondents on the issue of "frustration from a lack of progress": 52.8 percent of participants agree compared to 38.4 percent nonparticipants. Apparently this is a lesson learned from

Table 5.4 Reasons for Increased or Decreased Participation

Reasons as ordered by current participant positive response rate	Current participant	Current nonparticipant
	Reason to increase work with N.A.	*Reason to begin work with N.A.*
1. Solution of specific concern to me	93.8%	84.1%
2. Provide a useful service to community	90.4	86.8
3. Sense of contribution/helpfulness	76.4	71.9
4. Increased knowledge of community	73.1	75.1
5. Friendship with participants	70.8	69.7
6. Increased sense of responsibility	67.4	64.3
7. Enhanced personal/professional goals	45.7	44.8
8. Provide material benefits	37.0	39.3
9. Increased political influence	31.1	30.1
10. Increased status or prestige	22.8	22.4
	Reason to stop participation	*Reason to keep from participation*
1. Amount of time it takes	57.5%	54.9%
2. Giving up personal/family matters	52.8	50.0
3. Frustration from lack of progress	52.8	38.4
4. Energy and effort involved	32.1	32.3
5. Need to participate in meetings	26.0	27.9
6. Interpersonal conflict	21.9	15.1

Note:
See text for exact wording of question.

experience. If you have not been an active participant, you are less likely to realize the difficulty of actually achieving results. The only other difference of more than 3 percent between participants and nonparticipants, the issue of "interpersonal conflict," strikes the same theme: nonparticipants apparently do not have the same level of awareness as participants about the conflict that is inherent in any participation process.

We can also look at one further aspect of the difference in responses from participants and nonparticipants: the frequency of "yes" answers to all of the reasons combined. Do nonparticipants see fewer positives and more problems, and does that contribute to their nonparticipation? Apparently, as Table 5.5 indicates, the answer is no. The average number of "yes" responses to the ten "why participate" questions is almost identical for participants and nonparticipants: 6.05 versus 5.85, yielding a t-value that is not significant at the .05 level. The average number of "yes" responses to "why not participate" questions is slightly different: 2.40 versus 2.18 "yes" answers out of six questions,

Table 5.5 Number of Reasons for Increased or Decreased Participation

Number of positive responses out of ten reasons for increasing work or beginning to work with neighborhood association:

	Mean	Standard error	(N)
Current participants	6.046	+/–.133	(324)
Current nonparticipants	5.846	+/–.072	(1426)

Note:
t = value = 1.23 (DF 1748), not significant at the .05 level.

Number of positive responses out of six reasons to discontinue or keep from working with neighborhood association:

	Mean	Standard error	(N)
Current participants	2.401	+/– .088	(324)
Current nonparticipants	2.182	+/– .044	(1300)

Note:
t = value = 2.23 (DF 1622), significant at the .05 level.

a difference that is significant at the .05 level: but the nonparticipants give *fewer, not more* reasons not to participate. This is apparently a phenomenon derived from the nonparticipant's lower response rates to the two questions discussed above that deal with frustration and conflict.

Because the differences between participant and nonparticipant answers on these questions are relatively small, it makes sense to combine them to address our next question: does neighborhood strength, neighborhood demographics, or individual socioeconomic status have a significant effect on the reasons for participation and nonparticipation? It is clear from the next three tables that they do, to varying degrees.

The striking implication of Table 5.6 is that neighborhood strength has little bearing on this issue. In most cases, a strong neighborhood association has not changed the social dynamic of the neighborhood as a whole. Only two differences are marginally significant between respondents from well organized and poorly organized neighborhoods: "increased knowledge of the community" and "increased prestige." In both cases a little under 5 percent more of the respondents from poorly organized neighborhoods found these two reasons attractive than did respondents from well-organized neighborhoods. Perhaps participants in strong neighborhood groups have discovered that increased community knowledge and prestige do not necessarily result from active participation. The only difference in reasons for nonparticipation which approaches significance is the frustration issue again. This may be an indication that stronger neighborhood associations reduce the frustration required to participate. But then the first two nonparticipation responses on this table suggest that time pressures are even more of a concern in the stronger neighborhoods, although not significantly so.

Table 5.7, on the other hand, turns up quite a few differences between residents in low- and high-income neighborhoods. Residents of high-income neighborhoods are more likely to value the "solution of a specific concern" than are residents of low-income areas. Conversely, all of the more personal reasons to participate are held in significantly greater esteem by residents in low-income neighborhoods than in high-income neighborhoods. This strongly suggests that the immediate, direct, and personal gains from participation need to be emphasized to attract more people from these neighborhoods into the process.

Table 5.6 Reasons for Increased or Decreased Participation by Neighborhood Strength

Reasons as ordered by current participant positive response rate	Neighborhood strength		
	Low	High	Chi-Square
Reason to increase or begin work with N.A.			
1. Solution of specific concern to me	86.7%	88.2%	.67
2. Provide a useful service to community	88.0	87.1	.21
3. Sense of contribution/helpfulness	71.6	73.2	.39
4. Increased knowledge of community	76.8	72.4	2.94[a]
5. Friendship with participants	69.0	70.6	.39
6. Increased sense of responsibility	65.4	65.2	.00
7. Enhanced personal/professional goals	44.9	43.8	.15
8. Provide material benefits	39.1	36.7	.72
9. Increased political influence	30.3	28.3	.61
10. Increased status or prestige	23.7	19.3	3.42[a]
Number of cases for each question is between 1275 and 1289.			
Reason to discontinue or keep from working with N.A.			
1. Amount of time it takes	52.9%	57.2%	2.15
2. Giving up personal/family matters	49.9	52.5	.77
3. Frustration from lack of progress	43.3	37.8	3.48[a]
4. Energy and effort involved	32.3	30.5	.41
5. Need to participate in meetings	24.8	25.3	.05
6. Interpersonal conflict	15.4	15.7	.22
Number of cases for each question is between 1185 and 1190.			

Notes:

For derivation of neighborhood strength index see Table 3.5 and Appendices C and D. Low = index values 1 and 2; high = index values 3, 4, and 5.

a. Significant at better than the .10 level.

Table 5.7 Reasons for Increased or Decreased Participation by Neighborhood Socioeconomic Status

Reasons as ordered by current participant positive response rate	Neighborhood socioeconomic category			
	Low	Moderate	High	Chi-Square
Reason to increase or begin with N.A.				
1. Solution of specific concern to me	83.3%	86.2%	89.5%	6.45[a]
2. Provide a useful service to community	88.8	87.5	87.4	.31
3. Sense of contribution/helpfulness	74.5	72.4	73.9	.53
4. Increased knowledge of community	77.7	77.5	73.0	3.99
5. Friendship with participants	74.5	70.9	68.8	2.42
6. Increased sense of responsibility	75.1	64.4	63.8	9.25[b]
7. Enhanced personal/professional goals	55.8	45.4	40.4	14.79[b]
8. Provide material benefits	54.1	39.3	33.5	26.85[b]
9. Increased political influence	46.2	29.4	25.8	29.90[b]
10. Increased status or prestige	33.8	24.4	15.9	32.00[b]

Number of cases for each question is between 1443 and 1459.

	Low	Moderate	High	Chi-Square
Reason to discontinue or keep from working with N.A.				
1. Amount of time it takes	48.6%	56.2%	58.2%	5.20
2. Giving up personal/family matters	47.0	48.6	56.4	8.83[b]
3. Frustration from lack of progress	47.8	40.3	38.7	4.78
4. Energy and effort involved	37.2	30.8	32.5	2.55
5. Need to participate in meetings	27.5	26.1	26.7	.16
6. Interpersonal conflict	24.0	15.0	15.3	9.14[b]

Number of cases for each question is between 1322 and 1328.

Notes:

For derivation of neighborhood socioeconomic index see Table 3.7 and Appendix E. Low = index values 1, 2, 3; moderate = index values 4, 5, 6; and high = values 7, 8, 9, 10.

a. Significant at the .05 level.

b. Significant at the .01 level.

In looking at the reasons for nonparticipation on this table, there are only two significant differences, and both are counter to what one might expect. It apparently is the individual from a high-income neighborhood who is significantly more likely to be concerned about family and personal pressures than is the person from a low-income neighborhood. This casts doubt on the "she's too busy surviving to participate" theory. And it is the person from a low-income neighborhood who is significantly more likely to worry about conflict at the meetings—casting doubt on the "expand participation and you'll bring in all the aggressive authoritarian rascals" theory.

When we examine the individual-level socioeconomic breakdown in Table

5.8, we see very similar results to those of Table 5.7, with differences between high- and low-income people even greater than those for neighborhoods. The main distinction between the two tables is that another block of reasons for participation has been brought forward. Those reasons we found to express "more nebulous community-oriented or social values" are also found to be significantly different between low- and high-income respondents, with low-income people more likely to see each of them as a participation value. This could be very important for successful outreach, since many of these values are substantially easier to achieve on an individual level in the participation process than are the more material benefits highlighted earlier.

We have found, then, a rich potential for attracting community residents to the participation organization. The goal of a participatory democracy is not to

Table 5.8 Reasons for Increased or Decreased Participation by Individual Socioeconomic Status

Reasons as ordered by current participant positive response rate	Individual socioeconomic status			
	Low	Moderate	High	Chi-Square
Reason to increase or begin work with N.A.				
1. Solution of specific concern to me	78.6%	88.9%	92.3%	47.26[b]
2. Provide a useful service to community	84.8	89.8	87.8	7.04[a]
3. Sense of contribution/helpfulness	77.3	72.1	65.9	16.36[b]
4. Increased knowledge of community	79.8	76.9	64.9	32.26[b]
5. Friendship with participants	71.2	71.5	65.2	6.00[a]
6. Increased sense of responsibility	68.8	64.5	59.9	8.91[b]
7. Enhanced personal/professional goals	47.4	44.4	41.2	3.91
8. Provide material benefits	50.3	34.4	29.9	52.42[b]
9. Increased political influence	37.4	25.7	27.6	22.14[b]
10. Increased status or prestige	29.9	20.0	14.9	35.78[b]

Number of cases for each question is between 1684 and 1698.

Reason to discontinue or keep from working with N.A.				
1. Amount of time it takes	48.5%	56.4%	64.5%	24.43[b]
2. Giving up personal/family matters	45.3	50.8	56.9	12.50[b]
3. Frustration from lack of progress	45.1	39.6	39.3	4.75
4. Energy and effort involved	34.4	29.6	32.6	3.24
5. Need to participate in meetings	30.8	26.7	24.7	4.66
6. Interpersonal conflict	21.2	15.2	12.0	15.64[b]

Number of cases for each question is between 1569 and 1574.

Notes:

a. Significant at the .05 level.

b. Significant at the .01 level.

get everyone involved, or even to compete in numbers with the electoral process. The personal time and energy costs of participation are substantial—certainly more than voting once a year—and not everyone will be willing to incur those costs. Instead, this goal is better defined as offering a realistic opportunity to all, letting them make the choice for participation in each instance. Such an opportunity would mean, as we have seen in the four cities of this study, that many more people will choose to be involved in working through the details of solutions to complex social problems than the handful that can do so in a purely representative system.

Equally important to expanding the overall opportunity for involvement is improving the balance of interests reflected by those who do choose to participate. Each of the areas we have considered—the approach of Alinsky-style community organizations, the many facets of outreach embodied in the neighborhood participation process, and the reasons for participation and nonparticipation given by our survey respondents—suggests ways that an improved balance can be accomplished. There are no absolute barriers to participation, only matters of degree. If we can learn these lessons, and allocate scarce community resources accordingly, we can bring our communities substantially closer to the ideals of participatory democracy.

Chapter 6

The Policy Link

The previous two chapters have attempted to make the case that models for the core organizations of participatory democracy already exist in neighborhood and other grassroots organizations in our communities, and that models of outreach—while needing to be improved—also exist and can be strengthened to meet the demands of such a democracy.

We now take up the third necessary element: an effective link between decisions made by the participation core groups and the final policy that is implemented. The need for this link in any democracy is reflected in the last three of Dahl's conditions discussed in Chapter 2: alternatives chosen by the process displace alternatives with lesser support, the chosen policies are implemented, and implementation decisions are subordinate to the decisions arrived at through the participation process. Taken together, these three conditions imply that the coupling between citizen choices and final policy is, ideally, extremely strong, overriding any diversions for the sake of a separately perceived "public interest" or private interests along the way.

In a purely representative democracy, the link between citizens and policy can be seen as twofold: one link that is very strong, between the representative and the policy outcome; and a second link that is very weak, in terms of policy, between the citizen and the representative. The criteria we drew out of Pitkin's work in Chapter 2 can serve as a guide to strengthening this weak link. It is unacceptable to have a "representative" acting willy-nilly according to his/her own whims of the moment. We are compelled by these considerations to see representatives acting "in the interest" of their constituents, being responsive to them, and when acting at odds with their wishes, providing a good explanation.

In contrast, the second link of the participation core group, between it and the community, is very strong. As we saw in Chapter 5, it is not a representative link but a direct link to those who choose to participate. The challenge is not to reflect the point of view of those who choose not to participate, but instead to expand the opportunity for involvement so that all who do participate can voice their concerns with no intermediary involved. For these groups it is the first link, between them and the policy process, that is often tenuous. It is rare in the current state of American democracy for participatory groups to have real impact on any government policy. Agency advisory committees are usually just that—advisory—with the administrator quite free to listen to the group or not, and make whatever policy choice she would have made anyway. Even the grassroots groups of Kettering's Domestic Policy Forum and the Study Circles Resource Group, which, as we have noted, do such a good job of citizen deliberation on broad policy questions, have virtually no route to achieve policy impact.

Citizen advocacy organizations fall in between these two poles, with moderate links in both directions. Their link to the policy process is often focused on narrow areas where, through a combination of expertise, repeated contact with policymakers, and in some cases electoral campaign effectiveness, they can have substantial impact. And their link to some citizens—those who actively support them—is often quite strong, but those opposing or neutral to their positions have virtually no role to play. The limitations on the former link that prevent it from becoming stronger, however, are severe, due to two of the concerns we raised about these interest and advocacy groups in Chapter 2: the problems of legitimacy and cacophony. Because any one group's base is a tiny portion of the population, and because the only way policymakers have to sort out the resulting cacophony of voices is through a representative process not well designed for this task, the policymakers have little reason to take heed.

Party organizations do not serve to significantly improve upon these links. As we have argued in Chapter 2, the development of party platforms is only loosely related to election campaign themes; party discipline in America today is virtually nonexistent; and the officeholder generally pays only minimal attention to direct campaign promises, let alone the proud pronouncements of the platform. The 1994 Republican party cohesion under the banner of the "Contract With America" drew a great deal of attention, in part because it was so rare. And even to the extent that party cohesion does exist upon occasion, it nearly always takes a form that strengthens the first link, between a block of representatives and the final policy outcome, and does little for the second link, between citizens and their representatives.

The consequences of the weak combination of links between citizens and policy outcomes have led many commentators to express concern about the "decline of mediating institutions" in our society.[1] Some argue for a "return to church and family values," others for a "return to strong, responsible parties" as a remedy to these problems. But few have any concrete suggestions about how such institutions could actually work to tackle the major social and political issues of the twenty-first century.

If we envision that participation core groups can replace these missing mediating institutions and strengthen the citizen-policy connection, we need to ask: what are the conditions that must be met by these groups and their link to the final policy outcome to fulfill their roles in a participatory democracy? We will examine eight major issues involving internal decision making, dialogue between groups, multigroup decision making, recognition of the process, oversight, parochialism, cooptation and alienation, and connection to existing representative institutions.

Collective Decisions

The participation core groups need to be able to reach collective decisions on public policy.

It is characteristic of many small citizen groups dealing with problems of large import to treat their deliberations as merely informative. It is true on college campuses, where major public figures are brought in as speakers and received, understandably, as a means to increase individual awareness of national and global problems, not as a starting point for a decision-making process. It is also true, more curiously, in the community issues process of groups like the Kettering Fund and the Study Circles Resource Center. In the latter cases, the emphasis on group process and tracking of individual issue positions before and after the deliberations puts more of an emphasis on collective consensus-building. Overall, however, the forums still remain primarily in the realm of adult education rather than political or policy action. In church social action committees, community-based advocacy groups, local political party caucuses, and many other local citizen organizations, the need to reach decisions tends to be recognized more frequently. But the decisions typically involve immediate actions the group can take to deal with pressing social or political problems, rather than how their deliberations can mesh with those of other groups across the city, state, or country to form a consensus about long-range solutions.

The neighborhood associations in this study also engage in the latter decisions, but combine them with decision making in a specific policy context. Their immediate-action decisions deal with what they can do independently to solve a neighborhood problem—forming a crime watch, staging a neighborhood clean-up day, consulting with specific property owners about a public nuisance developing on their property. Their policy decisions deal with what they want the city to do: stepped-up agency enforcement, improved public services, revisions in the zoning code, a new ordinance for protecting the local water supply, and so on.

This hybrid approach may, in fact, be the most productive model for participation core groups. From their experience in hands-on work on day-to-day neighborhood issues, they gain a recognition of the reality of individual and community problems, and how much government programs can or cannot do to resolve them. This experience often carries over into a very practical style of policy consideration, avoiding the artificial idiosyncratic solutions often proposed by less grounded groups. For example, one Portland neighborhood became concerned about new multifamily housing a developer was proposing for its area. These concerns involved both the project's impact on the aesthetics of the neighborhood and practical concerns like parking, congestion, and so on. Instead of making this a black-and-white issue, as many such issues become, the neighborhood negotiated with the developer over their specific concerns, came up with guidelines for their resolution, shared these proposals with other neighborhoods, lobbied the city council, and eventually ended up with a new zoning category that could be used in many neighborhoods of the city. The new classification, enacted into the zoning code, allowed increases in density to be accompanied by a range of architectural and structural features that made the new buildings an enhancement rather than a detraction to the neighborhood.

Whatever their central focus, participants in the neighborhood associations recognize that a central mission is to confront community issues, reach a decision among themselves, and proceed to implement those decisions either on their own or with other community or governmental actors. Their greatest limitation is not on the quality of the decisions they make, but on the range of issues they feel empowered to tackle, a question we will take up shortly.

Inter-Group Dialogue

A dialogue needs to be maintained among the participation core groups to identify common ground and work out differences.

The more that the issues considered by participation core groups extend beyond their own geographic (or institutional) scope, the more important is an ongoing dialogue on those issues among the core groups. In considering issues that require changes in government policy or practice, the relevant issue is which level of government needs to implement the change. If the participation process is to gain the level of legitimacy now attained only by legislative institutions, all participation groups within the jurisdiction of that governmental body need to be involved.

Unfortunately, this dialogue is all too rare. Even in cities that have among the strongest participation systems in the country, such as the four cities of this study, we found that the neighborhood groups work independently far more often than they work together on an issue. The permanent coalitions in Portland and Dayton, each of which have their own staff and offices, helped to meet this problem on a limited geographic basis. But the most frequent roles of even these coalitions involve support for individual neighborhood activities, or joint efforts on immediate neighborhood problems they have in common, rather than on citywide public policy issues, or issues relevant on a larger scale. Proposals for an East Side freeway relocation in Portland, for example, brought together nearby neighborhoods to work out alternatives over a several-year period. And a fire in an inner-city paint factory in Dayton resulted in toxic pollutants seeping into the drinking water aquifer, uniting a dozen neighborhoods and environmental groups to develop new storage guidelines in the area of the aquifer.

The neighborhood coalitions in Dayton, more frequently than in the other cities, become involved in citywide issues. But most of these issues tend to be initiated by the city rather than the neighborhoods. When the school bond issue appeared to be in trouble, for example, the city called upon the coalitions to generate discussion in the neighborhood about its importance and ask for neighborhood support. Most of the neighborhood coalitions and their associated neighborhoods did agree to give their support, with a condition—that the schools immediately set up a participation system of their own. This agreement was reached, the bond issue won, and a system of community-based school councils was developed.

The reason that more of a neighborhood-to-neighborhood dialogue does not exist seems to be twofold: first, as we will discuss in the next section, the political dynamics in these cities make it difficult to do so; second, the mission of the neighborhood associations themselves makes this dialogue a relatively low priority on their agenda. This second explanation stems from the origins of the participation systems in each city and the development of their work over the past twenty-five years. In each city, the initial rallying cry that led to the organization of the neighborhoods as a citywide system was "let's build a better neighborhood." The people who were attracted to the organizations, particularly in leadership positions, were those who saw neighborhood issues—crime, housing, traffic, trash collection, and other problems whose impact was immediately visible from the windows of their homes—as the most important for their quality of life. Over the years, it is these issues with which the neighborhoods have had the greatest success and gained the greatest reputation. And thus it is a neighborhood-oriented mission that dominates nearly all of the groups.

As a result of this focus, issues which impact upon a much wider geographic scope tend to be seen as "somebody else's responsibility," even when neighborhood leaders recognize them as having important consequences for their own area. When "somebody else" does come along to organize an effort, the neighborhoods will often work with them, but they will rarely take the initiative themselves. In the Dayton paint factory issue mentioned above, for example, environmental organizations were dominant in the initial leadership. A similar direction of leadership, from the outside in, occurred during the time of our research in a proposal for a downtown Dayton arts complex, a coalition for the homeless in St. Paul, and a public utilities ownership initiative in Portland.

The effort to expand the neighborhood-to-neighborhood dialogue in these cities will not be easy. In Portland, for example, at least three major efforts to develop a formal citywide neighborhood coalition over the last twenty years have all failed. The most recent led to a citywide conference attended by more than 500 people in September 1993, but generated little follow-up organization. It is apparent that the starting point for such an expanded effort must rest with individuals within the neighborhood organizations who already see the need for citywide initiatives led by these organizations. The citywide network could begin with small working groups of these "leading lights" and gradually build from there.

Multi-Group Decision Making

The network of participation core groups needs to be able to reach decisions on the priority issues that emerge from the individual groups.

Beyond the expansion of cooperation and communication between the participation core groups, the logic of our discussion on participatory democracy demands that binding decisions emerge from the network of groups at the level appropriate to the governmental policy involved. Maintaining the value of face-to-face deliberation and decision making implies assemblies of the core groups at the city, state, and even national levels. This same value demands that each such assembly remain small enough so that every participant has a realistic opportunity to hear and be heard by all other participants on the issues before them—realistically, somewhere between a few dozen and a few hundred people. Some would argue that electronic networking would make such assemblies unnecessary. Without trying to tackle this whole issue here, suffice it to say that we must consider the implementation of electronic democracy at best a possibility that needs far more experimentation and development before it could be applied on a significant scale.

The recognition of the need for reasonably small, higher-level assemblies immediately brings us back to the question of representation. If not everyone from the lowest-level participation group—the neighborhood, for example—can realistically attend the assembly of the next-level participation group—at the city level, for example—the lower-level group must send "representatives" to the higher-level body. In such a process, all of Pitkin's conditions for representation—acting in the interest of those represented, being responsive to them, using a degree of independent judgment within the higher body, respecting the independent judgment of the lower bodies, and resolving conflicts of interest between the represented and representative—should be met as fully as possible. To maintain the participatory nature of the whole system, additional requirements are also essential. These requirements can perhaps best be summed up in a single additional condition: that the participants in the lower-level body be enabled to maintain their full involvement in an issue, at whatever level it reaches. This implies much greater communication between citizens and their representatives than is possible in existing representational structures. It also implies an iterative process, with the results of initial deliberations at the lower level being "sent up" to a higher level, and the concerns expressed by other representatives at that level being "sent back down" to the lower level for further discussion and compromise until a final decision can be reached. A final implication of this condition on representation is that the role of each representative be defined, limited, or expanded according to the desires of her constituency, up to and including the ability of that constituency to replace her whenever they so choose.

Forerunners of these networks exist in institutions as far-ranging as the national and state consensus process undertaken by the League of Women Voters through its local chapters—a very participatory process, but limited in scope[2]— and the platform processes that the national parties have at times attempted through their ward and town committees—a barely participatory process, but expansive in scope.[3] Such a network process obviously takes substantial time to implement and would be able to reach decisions on a limited range of issues—far fewer than a legislature takes up during the course of a year, for example, but far more than citizens can deal with during the election process.

Decision-making networks of any kind beyond the neighborhood or neighborhood coalition level are rare in the cities in this study. There are a wide array of citywide participation opportunities in each of the cities, but most are in the form of advisory committees, and most do not function as direct representatives of the neighborhood groups. In Dayton, for example, the only citywide body directly representing neighborhoods consists of a group of Priority Board (neighborhood coalition) leaders who meet monthly to help identify common problems and coordinate agendas and resource demands upon the city. In Birmingham, a citywide Citizens Advisory Board is composed of neighborhood delegates and is perceived by neighborhood leaders as a structure that allows neighborhood residents, particularly from black areas of the city, to have for the first time a direct communication link to city hall. But its scope is a very small part of the issues that the city, or even the neighborhoods, are dealing with, and most of its decisions relate to the operations of the neighborhood associations themselves.

St. Paul provides one of the few examples of neighborhood representatives gaining real control over major citywide decisions. Its Capital Improvement Budget committee (CIB) is composed entirely of neighborhood representatives (formally nominated by the neighborhoods and appointed by the mayor). The committee makes the initial decisions on all capital expenditures in the city, whether the funding source is federal, state, or local. Proposals are submitted to it by city agencies, individuals, and most often the neighborhood groups themselves. Nearly 70 percent of the projects funded are derived from proposals submitted by a neighborhood or neighborhood-agency joint effort. Each CIB member rates each proposal on an elaborate point system, the ratings are summed, and the committee then examines them in order of the resulting priorities, making specific allocation proposals as it goes. The proposals must be approved by the mayor and city council, but few are changed. The weakness of the system is in the ties back to the neighborhoods—the CIB members tend to lose their connection to the neighborhood groups, and operate almost as an independent "citizen jury" on budget issues.

The reason that citywide decisions are so rare in these communities seems to be rooted in the basics of political power: city councillors, almost to a person, continue to see themselves as the legitimate guardians of the citywide public interest. Their sense is that neighborhoods do a great job in their own areas, but that the appropriate balance is maintained when they, the councillors, weigh the citywide concerns against the neighborhood positions. Therefore, while the neighborhood associations individually and collectively have a tremendous influence on issues such as land use, neighborhood-scale development, crime prevention, and neighborhood environmental concerns, their ability to deal with citywide issues, including development projects affecting the economics of the entire city, is severely limited. Citywide convocations of neighborhoods to address the larger issues are not encouraged. This is true even in St. Paul, where a majority of the councillors were once officers of neighborhood organizations.

Overcoming these limitations would seem to require a grassroots political movement on a scale similar to those that began the neighborhood system in each city. There must be a broad citizen demand for an increased role of grassroots groups in the broader citywide issues before the status quo can change.

Legitimacy

> *The core groups, the decision-making process, and its outcomes need to be recognized and accepted by policymakers, administrators, and the public as a whole.*

The problems we reviewed in the previous section imply the need for a shift in political values to accompany the structural changes necessary to empower participatory organizations. It is clear that just such a change in values accompanied the initiation of the neighborhood systems in each of the cities in this study. At least several dozen strong neighborhood groups had existed in each of these cities, except Birmingham, for decades before the participation systems begin in the mid-1970s. But they did not have an accepted status or recognition as part of the political process until these systems were established. Generally, a major grassroots issue was part of the initiating process— the exclusion of blacks in Birmingham, a proposed freeway system in Portland, human services funding in Dayton. Outside pressures had a role: very directly in terms of federal community development funding requirements for racial balance and citizen participation in Birmingham, or indirectly in terms of the availability of massive transportation funds in Portland. And political leadership was ready: an energetic new mayor in Portland and St. Paul, a council in Birmingham that saw the writing on the wall.

These conditions led to a broad public perception in each city of the need for new mechanisms of citizen participation and control—of renewed connections between citizens and their government. The public acceptance, and even demand, for a new approach existed early in the process. Gradually policymakers and administrators also came to the conclusion that structural changes needed to be made. In each case, governmental recognition of the individual neighborhood groups and participation vehicles became part of the new system. This took the form of one or more city ordinances providing the basic structure, and specific guidelines and agency processes ensuring that the groups were responsive to their own communities (through ongoing elections in Birmingham and Dayton, and through formal group-by-group recognition in Portland and St. Paul).

It is this recognition process that has given the organizations and their decisions the legitimacy that they now enjoy. Their decisions are taken seriously, and generally acted upon, in a dozen realms of activity in as many city agencies (for instance, the Planning Departments, Zoning Appeals Board, Community or Economic Development Agencies, Public Works Departments, Transportation Departments, Recreation Departments, Police Departments, and so on). In every city office, the neighborhood maps are up on the wall, and the lists of neighborhood contacts are on the desks.

The conclusion that city officials listen is confirmed by our population survey, as Table 6.1 indicates. We asked the following question:

How do you think the people who run your city or town would react if you let them know about a major neighborhood problem you are having? If you explained your point of view to the officials, what effect do you think it would have? Would they give your point of view serious consideration, would they pay only a little attention, or would they ignore what you had to say?

The table shows the percentage of respondents in each neighborhood strength category that gave the most positive of the three answers—expecting serious consideration by officials. In an age of severe skepticism about government, these results are remarkably high in all neighborhoods—in the highest category, over 48 percent of respondents anticipated a serious government response. The differences between neighborhoods are, however, statistically significant at the .01 level. The relationship appears to be curvilinear with neighborhood strength: the neighborhoods at the lowest and highest end of the strength scale ended up with the highest expectations, and the lowest confidence occurred in the mid-strength neighborhoods. Apparently a little participation is a dangerous thing for public officials and expectations of responsiveness. Statistically significant differences in the perception of responsiveness do

Table 6.1 How Would Officials React to Citizen Concerns?

Neighborhood strength index value	Give serious attention	Pay little or no attention	(N)
Low 1	42.8 %	57.2 %	(313)
2	38.9	61.1	(645)
3	37.5	62.5	(715)
4	44.7	55.3	(575)
High 5	48.6	51.4	(177)

Pearson Chi-Square = 12.69, significant at the .01 level.

Exceptions

7	28.8 %	71.2 %	(66)
8	35.2	64.8	(54)

Note:
See text for exact question wording.

not arise when measured across individual SES levels or neighborhood economic variables.

Oversight

> *Once a decision is made and accepted, the participation core groups
> need to be able to oversee policy implementation.*

As pointed out in the eighth of Dahl's conditions (considered in Chapter 2), an important feature of a democracy is that implementation decisions remain subordinate to the democratic decision, or are subject to the same processes by which that decision was made. For our current purposes, this means that the same networks of participatory groups that make the decision need to receive a regular flow of information about how implementation is progressing, and must have an opportunity to respond if they perceive problems. This requirement underlines the necessity that the participation core groups and their related higher-level assemblies be ongoing organizations, not one-time political movements.

For the cities in the study, this oversight process works extraordinarily well. As we mentioned in Chapter 5, a regular flow of information does arrive at the doorsteps of the neighborhood groups in all the cities, either by informal arrangements developed over the years, or by formal requirement, as in St. Paul's Early Notification System. Many of the volunteer leaders and virtually all of the staff are in weekly if not daily contact with administrative agencies to ensure that specific projects are being implemented. We received very few complaints in our interviews with these leaders that city bureaucrats had blindsided them, promising one thing and delivering another.

The Dayton approach to oversight is particularly valuable. Every month each neighborhood coalition holds an Administrative Council attended by group of city staff people from as many as a dozen administrative agencies working on issues before the neighborhoods. The councils operate much like a candidates' night, with the candidates replaced by agency representatives. Each agency person stands before the neighborhood board and is asked questions, informed of new issues, congratulated on their response to the previous month's requests, or warned about problems in agency initiatives. The interchange helps to give the day-to-day operations of government a human face. It is not a great leap of faith to believe that if similar interchanges were a regular part of the interaction of citizens and *federal* agencies, major changes in levels of responsiveness and trust of these agencies would result.

Thinking Big, Thinking Whole

The big issues need to be confronted, and parochialism overcome.

On several occasions in this book, we have run into one of the most significant limitations upon the neighborhood groups we studied: the range of issues on which they typically work. In the discussion above, we posited that a major part of this problem is caused by a political dynamic that yields distrust of the neighborhood bodies by citywide officials. This distrust seems to focus more on the parochial perspectives of the neighborhood representatives than on their competence to examine the broader issues.

Parochialism does exist in these groups. But it is not limited to neighborhood participants. It exists in the perspective of any individual who has not grappled with the larger picture or been forced to confront the differing values of fellow-countrymen on a particular issue. And perhaps more important, it directly affects the outcomes of elections, and the roles of individual legislators, whether they be city councillors or U.S. Senators. For the elected official, a parochial attitude may be compounded by the range of political, party, funding, and legislative pressures that we listed in Chapter 2 that encourage the official to act other than entirely in the interests of his constituents or the national, state, or city interest.

The issue is not whether parochialism exists, or whether it influences the political process, but how best to overcome it. It is clear that involvement in community problem solving helps individuals to remove the blinders on their own perceptions. In *The Rebirth of Urban Democracy,* for example, our research team demonstrated that participation has a significant effect on a participant's tolerance toward differing positions and the attitudes of other community members.[4] In addition, the work of the Kettering Foundation and its Domestic Policy Forums has documented the changes in attitudes of participants grappling with major national policy issues from before to after the series of forum sessions.[5]

Participation efforts that have been developed by such agencies as the U.S. Corps of Engineers, the Environmental Protection Agency, the Forest Service, and the Food and Drug Administration also have demonstrated that average citizens can provide valuable input on the largest problems of the nation's water and power supplies, waste treatment, and agricultural and mineral resources when they are able to consult with experts of their own choosing, assess alternate values on their own terms, and work through the alternatives in a step-by-step process.[6] It is clear that neither the complexity of the major issues nor the backwardness of "laymen" is the limiting factor in a wider adoption of face-to-face citizen decision making. We are restrained instead by a lack of political will.

Standing Up

The process needs to be able to withstand the dual threats of cooptation by the bureaucracy and alienation from the bureaucracy.

A major criticism of the neighborhood associations we have examined is that they are overly dependent upon the very bureaucracies they are designed to oversee. These criticisms are not unlike those leveled at the legislative committees and regulatory agencies charged with becoming too friendly with the private interests they are supposed to regulate.

Administrators, on the other hand, worry that through the participation programs the cities are providing aid and comfort to "the opposition." They worry that the levels of alienation that currently exist mean that strong citizen participation will at best cause unending delay and conflict or at worst take a meat axe to their programs.

The truth lies somewhere in between. Anyone who has witnessed the long struggle in Portland over the guidelines for city-neighborhood relations cannot help but recognize the fierce independence that exists in these organizations. Yet most of the groups are far more willing to reach a compromise position with a government agency or developer than typical Alinsky-style community organizations (although some of the neighborhoods were originally organized by Alinsky's Industrial Areas Foundation or are currently members of confrontational networks like National People's Action).

On the cooptation side, the most serious concern is the substantial funding received by neighborhood groups or coalitions directly from city government. While many, especially the larger groups, raise some or most of their own funds, many others raise none at all. This is an issue that needs to be addressed as the organizations mature. Two directions are possible: more funds can be raised by small dues payments either contributed on an annual basis or, like ACORN, by passing the collection plate at every meeting. After all, if ACORN, which attracts some of the lowest-income participants of any community organization, is able to fund 45 percent of its budget through such donations, the average neighborhood groups should be able to do at least as well.

But the participation process we have been describing is unquestionably a civic function. And we expect to pay for civic functions through our tax base. Perhaps we need to look at direct allocation of tax revenues to neighborhood groups as an entitlement, not subject to the whims of agency budgeting. The idea is not entirely new—Senator Hatfield of Oregon introduced a tax check-off bill for neighborhood groups as early as 1975.[7] There is also some evidence that the political will exists to provide such funding: attempts to cut back support for the neighborhood associations at one time or another in all of the cities but Birmingham have consistently met with failure due to citizen uproar at the prospect. However they are funded, the control by participation core groups of their own staff and at least minimal communication resources is an essential part of their successful operation.

Addressing the issue of alienation, the data presented here and in *The Rebirth of Urban Democracy* clearly show that increased participation and stronger neighborhood associations tend to reduce the gap between citizens and their government, not increase it. Table 6.2 shows the explicit results of our survey questions about trust in government. It measures the difference in attitudes between trust in city government and trust in the federal government. As expected, far more people have greater trust in local government, at all levels of neighborhood strength. And, for both high- and low-income individuals the levels of trust increase significantly with neighborhood strength. The answer to alienation is to increase, not decrease, the strength and effectiveness of the participation organizations.

Table 6.2 Can Local Government Be Trusted More Often Than National Government to Do What Is Right?

Neighborhood strength index value	Percent who trust local government more than national government		
	Low SES	Moderate SES	High SES
Low 1	30.3%	41.1%	47.4%
2	35.3	41.8	38.9
3	40.6	39.8	38.7
4	33.9	42.5	47.2
High 5	38.8	45.3	67.6
(N)	(1022)	(982)	(555)
Pearson Chi-Square	12.88	3.58	22.12
Significance:	.12	.89	.005
Exceptions			
7	44.8%	18.5%	20.0%
8	54.2	73.5	58.8

Note:
Each figure represents the percentage of respondents in that neighborhood strength category who expressed a greater trust level when asked: "How much of the time do you think you can trust the government in [your city] to do what is right—just about always, most of the time, or only some of the time?" than when the same question was asked with [your city] replaced by Washington, D.C.

Democratic Connections

Constructive relationships between the participation group process and existing forms of representation need to be developed and maintained.

A practical participatory system is not a replacement but rather a complement to existing representative processes. Successful participation should be able to thrive on this reciprocal relationship rather than be disruptive to it or threatened by it. As we have noted, the participation groups are able to tackle issues in a way that legislators simply cannot. They are able to deal directly with the immediate ramifications of the issue in their own community. And they are able to take on a few policy issues in detail to broker differing values and perceptions among citizens. Angry citizens are not left on the outside shouting foul, but are brought into the process to at least begin to understand their differences and their common ground.

Even if the system of assemblies of participation core groups discussed above were in full operation, most of the issues currently on the legislative agenda would still be there. Only a few of the issues that generate the greatest interest and require the greatest attention of the citizenry would be within the capacity of the participation groups to tackle. Perhaps if such an approach had been in place during the health care debates of 1994, for example, we would not have been in the anomalous situation of a majority of citizens opposing the Clinton health plan as a package, while supporting most of its provisions when asked about them individually. Perhaps if the federal deficit were the subject of the participation process, we would not have such a large gap between the programs that people want to see continue and the taxes they are willing to pay for them.

The four cities of this study provide important examples of the likely relationship between the legislative body and the participatory organizations. In each city, a solid majority of city councillors strongly supported the system as a means of helping them do their work better. While a few had qualms about the neighborhoods forming "another layer of government," most felt that the groups were often on the front lines of issues and responding to day-to-day concerns of residents, enabling the councillors to spend more time on the larger issues that faced the city. In each city, the neighborhoods served as training grounds for elected officials and agency professionals alike. The mayors of both St. Paul and Portland at the time we were in these cities had originally entered the political sphere as neighborhood presidents.

From the citizen point of view, the legislators provide the professional stability and balance demanded by the thousands of issues the legislature must deal with every year. While these cities have not progressed to the point where the neighborhood associations deal with citywide issues on a regular basis, citizens express a high degree of confidence that the city councillors will respond to the associations on these larger issues as well as on the neighborhood issues that are directly within the organizations' responsibility.

Of the three essential components of participatory democracy—the deliberations and decisions of the core grassroots groups, their outreach to all citizens in their area, and their relationship to the policy process—it is this policy link that is the least proven and most controversial. Nevertheless, our analysis has shown that many of the necessary conditions for this link have been tested in the neighborhoods and city governments of Birmingham, Dayton, Portland, and St. Paul. The groups make clear policy decisions for their own neighborhoods, are recognized in these areas by the city's elected and administrative officials, stand up well against cooptation and citizen alienation, and have a substantial impact on public policy in their communities. They are limited, however, in the type of issues they can address successfully and in their formal decision-making powers at the citywide level and beyond. Their greatest challenge, and ours, is the development of a stronger network of participatory organizations able to take on the largest issues faced by our society today.

Chapter 7

Further Explorations

Despite the expansion of individual rights and entitlements in recent decades, Americans find to their frustration that their control over the forces that govern their lives is receding rather than increasing . . . there is a widespread sense that we are caught in the grip of impersonal structures of power that defy our understanding and control.

This condition raises with renewed force the plausibility of republican concerns. The republican tradition taught that to be free is to share in governing a political community that controls its own fate. Self-government in this sense requires political communities that control their destinies, and citizens who identify sufficiently with those communities to think and act with a view to the common good. . . . Whether self-government in this sense is possible under modern conditions is at best an open question.

—Michael Sandel, *Democracy's Discontent*

The possibility of self-government is the question we have struggled with throughout this book. Our focus has been on a type of organization that embodies in its nature the face-to-face deliberations that seem to have vanished in so many other spheres of American activity, yet are often seen as essential for effective self-government. Do such organizations have a role in the future of democracy?

We have argued that if they do, three elements are critical to this role: the strength and openness of the participation organizations themselves, their continuing link to the community, and their effective link to government policy making. These elements can be measured and tested in the context of urban governments that have committed themselves to broad-based citizen participation in their governance, and with the neighborhoods through which they have largely fulfilled this commitment.

We have discovered that strong neighborhoods succeed where many other political structures fail: in their ability to generate significant levels of citizen participation. As measured through the basic characteristics of the 273 neighborhoods in our study, neighborhood strength is highly correlated with individual participation measures, reaching 37 percent in the strongest neighborhoods studied. Many of these participants might simply have attended one neighborhood event during the year, but many others were active in meetings, committees, and events on a monthly basis or even more often.

This participation runs across the board in neighborhoods ranking both high and low in socioeconomic status, even while participation remains highly correlated with individual socioeconomic status. The difference in participation from what one would normally expect based on individual socioeconomic status is significantly correlated with this measure of neighborhood organizational strength.

These organizations fulfill many of the requirements of a core participation group quite well, but fall short on other requirements. They do a good job of representing all segments of the community, rich and poor, black and white, and of many and varied interests, at the expense of representing any one segment optimally. While they are generally open to new participants, they are particularly vulnerable to ossification over time and need substantial incentives from both internal and external sources to regularly rejuvenate themselves.

The organizations are especially good at fostering both an egalitarian and a deliberative atmosphere. They are able to tackle any and all issues that arise and are better at being open to a wide range of issues and points of view than most other citizen groups. They clearly allow citizens to "insert an issue onto the political agenda" more readily than does the electoral or representative process.

In these four highly participatory cities, the neighborhoods all have an ongoing relationship with a fairly strong support network that allows the organization to prosper through good times and bad, with basic funding for staff support, offices, newsletters, and the like. At a citywide level, this can work where there is a strong commitment to neighborhood associations across the city and across the departments of government. To work on a higher level, the same type of commitments would be needed from governors and presidents, congresspeople, and heads of the relevant state and federal departments.

Without such commitments, one of the greatest limitations of these organizations is the restricted geographic scope of their issues. Other types of organizations often are able to muster greater enthusiasm and political clout on other concerns—such as development of environmental regulations, production of affordable housing, or the politics of health care—when the issues extend to the whole city, and certainly when advanced to the state or the nation. Despite a resurgence of interest in neighborhood-level organizing during the last thirty years, effective national, state, or even congressional district coalitions of neighborhood groups have been rare and fleeting.

Effective outreach is a very intensive, resource-hungry process. Many of these neighborhood organizations do it well, but not nearly as well as many Alinsky-style organizations within their usually more limited segments of a community. The information flow to and from interested residents is one of the areas where neighborhoods work best—in part because city government demands they take this role seriously as part of the city's recognition of them as representatives of the whole community. They generally do a much better job of keeping citizens aware of city government events than any government agency does on its own. And they do succeed in making it easy for the voices of any residents who take the time to drop by a local meeting to be heard at city hall.

A significant failing of the neighborhood groups, in comparison with other community-based organizations, is in marshaling resources to meet crises that extend beyond the limits of any single neighborhood. Much of their energy is directed toward day-to-day issues, often including work on underlying causes; but that leaves little energy to make single issues a life-or-death organizational cause the way Alinsky-style organizations often do. We have been able to identity a number of ways for neighborhood groups to increase their outreach and participation, including taking some pages from Alinsky-style organizations, without abandoning their own mission; paying attention to specific, concrete benefits for participants as well as to broad community values; and focusing on ways to minimize the strains due to conflict and frustration in the participation process.

The third component of our democratic model, the link between the neighborhood organizations and broader policy outcomes, is not strong. To the extent that policy is made for issues within a single neighborhood, the groups have a high recognition by political, administrative, and even economic leaders, and they play a dominant role. But their relationships to and recognition by governmental structures outside the city are typically very weak. The dialogue among neighborhood groups, even in different parts of the same city, tends to be infrequent and inconsequential. Nevertheless, the group's oversight of policy implementation—as it affects the neighborhood—works extraordinarily well. Extensive interaction with public officials, often with the neighborhoods taking the lead in such forums as Dayton's Administrative Councils, contributes in significant ways to increased governmental responsiveness and the perception of such responsiveness by citizens.

The neighborhood groups in our study are not coopted, nor are they alienated from the sources of local political power. There tends to be a mutual recognition by city policymakers and citizens of the important role each has to play in the process. They are not parochial in the sense that they tend not to promote narrow interests or perspectives within their sphere of action. But they are parochial in the sense that their range of issues is very local, and their connections to larger democratic processes are limited.

If we look back on our discussion of representation in Chapter 2, we can see that the neighborhood groups are, in fact, excellent representatives of the people in their neighborhoods from both the purely participatory and purely representative points of view. Our evidence is strong that they do act in the perceived interest of the represented and are very responsive to them. As representatives they do take action on behalf of those who are represented, and in close concert with them—much more so than representatives on any larger scale. The neighborhood organizational perspective almost always sees their constituents as capable of taking independent action, and depends directly upon their judgment. Any conflicts between the organization as representative and those it represents tend to be resolved quickly and decisively.

Questions of Scale

We can conclude that strong neighborhood organizations make for good representation. Why, then, are they so seldom considered seriously as a cornerstone of democracy? The answer is immediate: we have long grown accustomed to the old saw that "village" or "Athenian" democracy is no longer possible when our polity has grown to the size of the nation. If all the people can no longer meet together in the same hall, then, of course, some other form of government must take their place.

The fallacy of this easy explanation is that our decision to abandon neighborhoods, town meetings, and other forums where people can directly deliberate, in favor of faraway councils, legislatures, and congresses, embodies only one solution to the challenge, the one of distant representative democracy to which we have all grown so accustomed. But why does the inability of all the people to meet together at the same time and the same place prevent them from meeting in different groups, in different places, and perhaps at different times? When they do so meet, are they no longer capable of the kinds of discussion and deliberation by which they used to run their towns? Are the political problems to be addressed of a totally different character than they were when people ran their own affairs? Are the difficulties of combining the results from multiple loci of deliberation so difficult that distant representation is so obviously preferable?

At a time when our representative democracy seems to be in such trouble, it may greatly benefit us to revisit these ideas and explore our alternatives to the questions of scale. We have found in this book that one type of participatory core group functions well in the framework of democracy, save for the limitation on its range of issues. We have found that its link to the community is far superior to that of most other representatives we have encountered. But we have also found that its link to the larger policy process and to a network of deliberation is almost nonexistent.

The questions that invite further exploration, therefore, both by academics and by political and community leaders, include the following:

1. How can the link between the policy process and the face-to-face deliberative bodies of ordinary citizens be improved? What structures would work, between the town meeting and the distant representative? What are the fundamental advantages and limitations of such structures? We have grown so accustomed to thinking of representation as a single-stage process that we have neglected the possibility of chains of representation in which groups of representatives are themselves represented to a larger body. If coupled with a deliberative process at each stage, and with constant feedback moving both up and down the chains as part of the deliberative process itself, how far would a two- or three-stage representative process take us in meeting the questions of scale?

2. How can and do ordinary citizens handle the "big issues" in the context of a deliberative process? Is it true that the complexity of our society and our technology has advanced so far that the character of political decisions has made the participatory process obsolete? As Michael Sandel noted in the last pages of his book, from which the opening quotes to this chapter were taken:

Self-government today . . . requires a politics that plays itself out in a multiplicity of settings, from neighborhoods to nations to the world as a whole. Such a politics requires citizens who can think and act as multiply-situated selves.[1]

How do our citizens measure up to these requirements? Who are the experts that can guide deliberating citizens through these complexities, and what relationships need they have to the citizen deliberators? Can citizens cope?[2]

3. Since the interests of citizens extend far beyond any geographic boundaries—whether they be neighborhoods, cities, or congressional districts (or, for that matter, states and nations)—how can citizens deliberating together in

nongeographic groups become a more productive part of the governmental process? There are many local chapters of larger organizations where these kinds of face-to-face deliberations take place today: in unions, the Alinsky-style community organizations of the Industrial Areas Foundation, ACORN, and National Peoples Action, Common Cause, and the League of Women Voters, plus tens of thousands of single-issue groups from the far left to the far right of the political spectrum and everywhere in between. How can the interaction of such organizations through government lead to resolution instead of gridlock? How can their roles in government become part of a one-person-one-vote democratic framework? Can representation occur directly within specific issue areas as well as through multi-issue representatives? Can citizens' membership in specific-issue organizations come to count politically in the same way that their residence in a specific Congressional District counts today?

A little participation is a dangerous thing. Evidence from our studies and others has indicated that a curvilinear relationship often exists between participation and attitudes such as trust, confidence, and frustration with and alienation from the governmental process. People who are way out of the loop, who don't connect with the governmental process at all, are often more trusting and less frustrated with government than those who have had a brush with governmental deliberations and gone away mad. People who are actively involved on a regular basis are also much more trusting and less frustrated than the average citizen. Perhaps some of the disillusionment we see with government in twenty-first century America is a product of citizens having greater awareness of happenings at the statehouse and the White House than they ever used to, but fewer opportunities to do anything about it. If a civil society is an antidote to our problems, then the elements of civil society that empower citizens to become part of the decision-making process are among the most vital forms of voluntary association. The solution to the problems of democracy may indeed be a little more democracy.

Appendix A

Characteristics of Surveyed Cities

Citywide Demographics

	Birmingham	Dayton	Portland	St. Paul
Population	288,611	193,536	375,897	270,230
Age				
Median age	29.6	28.1	31.4	29.5
65 or over	13.6 %	11.8 %	15.3 %	15.0 %
17 or under	26.8 %	27.4 %	21.8 %	24.1 %
Minorities				
Black	54.7 %	36.9 %	7.6 %	4.9 %
Other minorities	0.5 %	1.1 %	6.0 %	5.0 %
Hispanic	0.8 %	0.9 %	2.1 %	2.9 %
Education				
h.s. graduate	60.9 %	59.3 %	75.8 %	72.4 %
college graduate	13.4 %	10.4 %	22.1 %	19.8 %
Housing				
owner occupied	53.2 %	50.6 %	53.3 %	55.7 %
Median value	$31,700	$28,300	$54,800	$52,900
Economic Status				
persons in poverty	21.6 %	20.8 %	13.0 %	10.9 %
Median family income	$15,437	$15,292	$19,501	$20,743

Note:
All figures are based on 1980 data from the United States Census Bureau.

Political Structure

	Birmingham	Dayton	Portland	St. Paul
Structure	Strong mayor	Council-manager	Commission	Strong mayor
Mayor	Elected separately 4-year term	Elected separately 4-year term	Elected separately 4-year term	Elected separately 2-year term
Council	9 seats	5 seats (including mayor)	5 seats (including mayor)	7 seats
	By district 4-year term	At large 4-year term (overlapping)	At large 4-year term (overlapping)	By district 2-year term

Appendix B

Neighborhood Participation Structures in Four Cities

This appendix provides an overview of the major features of the citywide neighborhood participation systems in Birmingham, Dayton, Portland, and St. Paul. Each description is organized into five categories:

A. Beginnings and Authorization
B. Neighborhood Structures
C. Citywide Citizen Structures
D. Outreach to Citizens
E. Other Major Program Components
F. Overall Perspective of the City on Citizen Participation

Birmingham Participation

A. Beginnings and Authorization

Born: October 15, 1974
Place: In City Council Resolution formally adopting the Citizen Participation Plan

The Birmingham participation system grew out of an extremely tense racial atmosphere following a decade of racial strife. In 1972, a Community Development Department was created, the first in a city with a tradition of among the lowest levels of per capita public expenditures in the country. At this time, the federal Department of Housing and Urban Development was promulgating strict guidelines for participation in a number of cities with past records of racial discrimination, one of which was Birmingham. The regional director for HUD outlined minimum requirements for involvement of the poor to Birmingham's mayor in July 1973.

In response to HUD's requirements, the Community Development Department proposed its first version of a participation plan in October 1973, and shortly thereafter a Community Resources Division was set up, which apparently began to implement the plan in several North Birmingham neighborhoods early the next year. The plan drew major protest from black leaders, particularly over its dependence upon a private organization, Operation New Birmingham, as the primary organizer of the neighborhood structure. This protest culminated with 500 people at a public hearing on the plan in the municipal auditorium on April 1, 1974. The official record notes that "almost all speakers expressed opposition to aspects of the initial plan." Staff listened to tapes from the hearing, conducted a workshop for more than 130 participants, and developed a revised plan which received final Council approval in October. The new plan omitted Operation New Birmingham from its provisions, and was generally well received.

At this point the program was off and running at full speed: an election of Neighborhood Citizens Committees was held in November 1974 to fill 258 positions, and neighborhood committees and advisory groups were subsequently formed. A major effort to inform the public about these groups was taken through flyers and posters, churches, community schools, radio and television announcements, and special events. The first meeting of the citywide Citizens Advisory Board (CAB) was held a few months later in February of 1975. The CAB specifically decided to adopt a citywide perspective, avoid partisan politics, and work cooperatively with city officials. Disposition of the $5 million Community Development Block Grant (CDBG) was the major CAB issue during this year. And it was important for this biracial, grassroots group of people simply to meet on a regular basis with the mayor and city council members.

B. Neighborhood Structures

1. Neighborhood Associations and Community Advisory Committees

At the heart of the Birmingham system are its ninety-three Neighborhood Associations. Like Dayton, but unlike Portland, the entire city is divided into defined neighborhoods. Except for newly annexed areas, the number and definition have remained fairly constant (up from eighty-four neighborhoods when the system began in 1974). Neighborhood population ranges from 180 to 8,200. The median neighborhood population is 2,740.

Two to six neighborhoods are grouped together into a community. A total of twenty-two communities exist. The members of the Community Advisory Committee (CAC) are the officers of the neighborhoods involved. They elect their own officers and representatives to the CAB. In practice, the CAB representation is the primary function of this community structure, although the CACs are required to meet at least bimonthly.

One representative from each of the twenty-two communities makes up the CAB. It is designed to present the opinions and feelings of the neighborhoods to city hall. (See below under citywide structures, C1, for further description of the CAB).

The rules of operation for the neighborhoods and higher-level structures are contained in the Citizen Participation Plan (CP Plan), which was in existence since the system's beginning. The provisions of this plan formally supersede any CAB, community, or neighborhood bylaws. Part of the agreement with citizens was that this plan would be reviewed and revised as necessary every two years. Major revisions did, in fact, occur on three occasions: October 12, 1976, July 5, 1978, and August 26, 1980. Elections for neighborhood officers changed from an annual to a biannual basis after 1976. The 1980 changes included combining the Community Resources Division and the Planning Division of the Community Development Department.

Voting membership in the neighborhood associations is open to any resident 16 years of age or older. Property owners, businesses, and other organizations may NOT be voting members.

The Citizen Participation Plan specifically states that neighborhood associations may go to the Community Development Department, the CAC, the CAB, or directly to other city departments and personnel. In practice, the Community Development Department has—at some stages in its history—discouraged neighborhoods from "circumventing" its control, insisting that all Community Resource Officers take issues through the central office of the Community Resource Division, not to other city departments directly.

The CP Plan also calls for Neighborhood Advisory Groups to be chosen by the neighborhood president, representing local organizations and specially disadvantaged groups. We found no evidence that these groups currently take an active role in the Birmingham system.

2. Elections

Key links between citizens and the city in Birmingham are the elections for officers of the neighborhood associations (called "selections" because of state law complications). The president, vice president, and secretary of each neighborhood must be chosen every two years at the polls in a September/October election held separately from municipal elections. Any Birmingham resident age sixteen or over may vote, and any resident age eighteen or over who has lived in the neighborhood for ninety days and attended at least two neighborhood meetings is eligible to run for office (by completing a declaration of candidacy). Any ties are resolved at the next neighborhood meeting. The elections are run by the Community Resources Division.

A typical turnout citywide is from 7,500 to 8,500 voters, and this has remained fairly constant over the last four elections. The highest turnout was in the second year of operation, 1975, with 11,654 voters. In some neighborhoods, turnout may run as high as 70 percent. More typically, turnout in a heavily contested election will run 10 percent to 15 percent of the voting age population. Uncontested elections may draw only 1 to 3 percent. In 1986, there were at least 309 candidates running for these offices.

3. Drawing Neighborhood Boundaries

At least half of the first year of the Birmingham CP system was devoted to identifying neighborhood and community boundaries. A team of city staff literally started at one end of the city, working its way to the other end, knocking on doors and asking people how they perceived their own neighborhood. Charles Lewis, locally known as "Mr. Citizen Participation," argues strongly that this process was critical in acceptance of the CP system: "When the program began, feeling by some citizens' groups for city officials included misunderstanding, antagonism, and distrust. When the new map was prepared which . . . changed the boundaries in accordance with citizens' recommendations, an important step was taken in establishing a trust relationship and two-way communication between citizens and city officials."

Like the Participation Plan itself, the boundaries were specifically left open for revision every two years. Few changes have been made, however, except to add neighborhoods from newly annexed areas.

4. CP Administrative Funding

No direct administrative funds are given to neighborhood associations (but see under the Neighborhood Allocation Process below for the large amounts of development money that have been spent on projects designated by the associations).

The administrative budget for the system is allocated primarily to the Community Resources Division of the Community Development Department. Up until 1987 almost all of the funds for the participation system apparently came from the Community Development Block Grant (CDBG) from the federal government. Approximately $500,000 is spent for the citizen participation system from this grant, including $94,000 for neighborhood communications. In addition, $158,000 was allocated directly to Neighborhood Services, Inc., an independent citizen group working in some of the lowest-income neighborhoods in the city.

5. Offices and Staffing

There are no neighborhood offices. Staffing for the Birmingham participation system is provided in its entirety by the Community Resources Officers who work out of the city hall office of the Community Resources Division. There were nine full-time officers in 1987, including the Principal Community Resource Officer, who serves as staff director for the system. There had been as many as thirteen full-time staff at its peak, and as few as six or seven when the program began.

6. Neighborhood Activities

The neighborhood officers tend to be like ward heelers for their neighborhood, taking the lead in many community events from housing rehabilitation to Halloween parties. And like ward heelers, they have an important material incentive to disperse—not patronage, but community projects. Large sums of development money, which have been as much as $70,000 a year for a neighborhood of 5,000 people, are allocated by the neighborhood organizations. Determination of how this money would be spent was a major factor that early organizers of the project felt would make citizens willing to commit the time and energy to participate.

Some individual neighborhood officers spend huge amounts of time on major neighborhood projects—from the housing rehabilitation corporation of North Pratt to the commercial development activities of Five Point South. The neighborhoods seem to be taking a more and more active role in zoning and land use kinds of decisions through the early warning they get of them. We witnessed neighborhood meetings with prospective developers that made it clear that developers realize they have a real stake in talking to the appropriate neighborhood associations before attempting to get zoning variances or other special agreements from the city.

Another major effort of neighborhoods has been the work to develop a community identity through a number of self-help projects and festivals. Tool-lending libraries have often been part of this. These have been very important in establishing a sense of community in many areas where no grassroots organizations had ever existed before.

C. Citywide Citizen Structures

1. Citizens Advisory Board

Taking the opposite approach from Portland's multiple channels of participation, Birmingham has one central body that channels policy proposals from neighborhoods into city hall: the Citizens Advisory Board. This body maintains contact with the mayor and the city council, as well as other departments when necessary. Its formal representative structure, derived from the neighborhood associations, gives it the potential to articulate policy positions as the voice of the neighborhoods.

The CAB meets monthly, and at least one meeting each quarter is mandated to be with the mayor and with the city council. CAB committees have been developed that largely parallel the city council committees. In 1986–87, for the first time, the three officers of the CAB were all black, a fact that caused a degree of concern among some of the white neighborhood officers. The CAB itself holds strongly to its effective operation as a biracial body. In fact, other observers have noted that is was only the second such body associated with local government in the history of the city (the first was the board of the local poverty program). A major question exists, however, about the impact of the CAB. It has no staff other than that of the Community Resources Division. It initially served a vitally important role of simply establishing contact, on a biracial basis, between people in the neighborhoods and the highest levels of government. Now that contact is an accomplished fact, however, the policy role of the CAB is unclear. They can and do offer advice, but it is not clear who listens under what circumstances, or what procedures exist for translating that advice into policy. The CAB seldom seems to take positions on major policy issues facing the city, and seldom seems to win when it does.

D. Outreach to Citizens

1. Monthly Neighborhood Newsletters

One of the most impressive and distinctive features of the Birmingham CP system is that the Community Resources Division mails out city and neighborhood information packets every month to every household in the city. Each neighborhood association can include whatever material it wishes in the mailing. The material typically includes meeting notices, new program descriptions, and information about other events or services of the city or neighborhood. This is a crucial method of making citizens aware of the role of the participation system and of their opportunity to participate.

2. Neighborhood Surveys

According to the city's description of program history produced in 1984, "Approximately 20 neighborhoods have completed or are in the process of completing systematic door-to-door surveys to identify neighborhood needs and problems." This information was to be used for neighborhood plans. We have found no evidence, however, that full population surveys have been used in policy decisions by either administrators or neighborhood leaders.

3. 'Cross Town *Newsletter*

A publication called *'Cross Town* was an important source of communication between and about neighborhoods for several years. It was typically a four-page newsletter that provided information about ongoing city programs, reported events important for the citizen participation system, and described recent activities of selected neighborhoods. The publication was discontinued in 1987 because of budget cuts.

E. Major Program Components

1. Neighborhood Allocation Process

The most direct policy input within the Birmingham participation system is the ability of neighborhood associations to determine how their allocation of capital development funds will be spent. This policy began in the first years of the system, when a formula was developed that allocated to each neighborhood a specific percentage of the CDBG funds coming to the city. The formula is based on population and neighborhood need. In 1987 and 1988, however, as increasing amounts have been cut out of this budget, each neighborhood was given a flat minimum amount. While in the early years between $6,000 and $70,000 was allocated to each neighborhood, the allocation in 1988 was down to a little over $3,000.

Each neighborhood allocation is made each year, even if no active neighborhood association exists at that time. During the year, each active neighborhood association votes to determine how this allocation will be spent. When a new association is formed, it has access to all the funds allocated during the inactive period. While neighborhoods clearly can spend for innovative projects they have developed, the city also becomes quite involved, in practice. What seems to happen sometimes is that the city will say to a neighborhood, "We have this new project ready to go in your area, do you want to spend your neighborhood allocation on this project?" Apparently most of the neighborhood allocations are spent on tasks performed either by city employees or contractors going through the usual city contract process.

2. Neighborhood Training Sessions

The Division of Community Resources provides orientation sessions for neighborhood officers after each election. In recent years, these have become opportunities for each new officer to get to know some of the heads of city agencies, and to learn how to go about making requests for basic services or policy changes.

Neighborhood Services, Inc., also provides leadership training for the neighborhood organizations within its area. There are thirty-two neighborhoods in some way connected with them, but only five or six seem to be involved in the core of their work.

3. Operation New Birmingham

One of the first organizations assigned to work on citizen participation in Birmingham was Operation New Birmingham (ONB). This group was a coalition of business and religious leaders that helped to promote more racially open economic and governmental processes in some of the hottest periods of the civil rights movement. They were given a contract in February 1974, apparently to implement the citizen participation plan, but their involvement was eliminated with the defeat of the original plan.

ONB is now the primary contract agency for the city assigned to manage downtown development. This practice is unusual compared to the operations of most cities we have examined—in general, economic development issues and downtown development are an important role of line departments of the city, and are not assigned, in as high a degree as we found in Birmingham, to a non-governmental body. In addition to this economic development role, ONB continues to be an important forum for interaction of black and white residents on questions of race relations and improving community life.

4. Neighborhood Services, Inc.

In 1979, a coalition of low-income groups organized by Greater Birmingham Ministries sued the city for failing to give low-income neighborhoods their fair share of CDBG funds. At issue was the city's "triage" system of rating neighborhoods that left out the most needy areas, which were judged to be lacking in leadership or resources necessary to make good use of the funds. Through this suit the coalition succeeded in obtaining an agreement from the city to allocate a substantially larger share of these funds to the lowest-income neighborhoods.

As a consequence of this action, thirty-two neighborhoods formed a coalition called Neighborhood Services, Inc. As of 1983, they had eight full-time staff people. They have continued to work on a number of development projects, from new housing to development of a community-based supermarket. They also maintain a continuing leadership development training program to help residents of these low-income neighborhoods to recognize and articulate their community's needs and take effective action to address those needs.

5. Neighborhood Information

The Division of Community Resources has the primary role of informing neighborhood presidents about events and decisions in city government that are relevant to their neighborhoods. A major part of this task is accomplished through a biweekly mailing, which includes information on such issues as:

- Requests for liquor licenses, pool tables, and dance permits
- Proposed zoning changes, and corresponding public hearing dates
- Community development projects undertaken by the city that will affect their neighborhood
- Notification of responses by the city to requests made by neighborhood officers
- Citywide notices including City Council agenda, public hearing notices, notification of board and staff vacancies to be filled by the City Council, agenda of the Planning Commission, Subdivision Committee, Zoning Advisory Committee, and the Zoning Board of Adjustments, and agendas and minutes of the CAB

The Division also has the responsibility to maintain the "official map of neighborhoods," the "official copy of the officers names and addresses," and the schedule of regular times and locations for neighborhood association meetings. The telephone number given in all city publications for contact with the neighborhoods and the participation system is the Division of Community Resources number.

6. Other Projects and Events

An important effort of the Birmingham system: they have sent dozens of neighborhood association officers to meetings of Neighborhoods, USA, and other neighborhood-based conferences to find out how other neighborhoods worked around the country. They have done this on a larger scale than any other city, as far as we know.

A major program supervised by several neighborhoods is the house-painting program, through which unemployed youth in the summer months are matched with homeowners who cannot afford to pay for repainting on their own. The neighborhood associations determine which homes are the highest priority and assign supervisory volunteers to get the job done.

F. Overall Perspective of the City on Participation

The Birmingham participation system was designed to create a sense of community in a shattered city. It brought blacks and whites together in a common vision for the future for the first time. Its focus was on physical development that had been badly neglected in years past. The Citizen Participation Plan represented the city's recognition of "the need and desirability of involving its citizens more directly and continuously in its community development efforts." Personal contact between city hall and average citizens of all colors and incomes was a cherished goal.

The Participation Plan has already accomplished many of its objectives. But it retains the focus upon central control with which it began: offices, staff, elections, and communications all emanate from city hall. Increasing ties between citizens and officials, not establishing independent citizen operations, has been the central focus. Unlike Portland, for example, there is a greater sense of a single channel for participation and a single source of support for it. This makes for a more coherent participation system, but also a more restricted one.

The system was also set up with a great concern for equal access, and the detailed electoral structure and formal representation through the CAB have performed this function well from the very beginning. Similarly, a lack of information for citizens had been a critical problem, again solved quickly and surely with the Birmingham system of monthly mailings to every household.

The biggest question that remains, now that these initial concerns have been met, is whether the system can coexist with a more pluralistic political system and gain a financial commitment from the city's general fund in the face of severe cutbacks in the federal monies that had been the mainstay of the participation effort.

Dayton Participation

A. Beginnings and Authorization

Born: 1971

Place: In the Planned Variations application to the federal government as part of the Model Cities Program

The original Model Cities program got underway in Dayton in 1967. In 1971, the Planned Variations proposal was approved, and the Priority Boards were formally initiated. In 1975, the City Commission passed an Informal Resolution making the Priority Boards the official voice of Dayton's neighborhoods. This resolution cited the positive experience of neighborhood councils, the Model Cities Planning Council, and the City Wide Priority Board system as having "demonstrated the worth and need for citizen participation." The city specifically wanted to authorize these boards as the participation mechanism to comply with federal guidelines for the Community Development Program.

Apparently 1975 was the year when Priority Board offices ("site offices") were first established throughout the city. It was also the year that the mail balloting process was first used in two Priority Board areas (see below). By 1980, all six residential Priority Boards used this method of balloting. The recognition of neighborhood group representatives in the Southeast Priority Board required a special resolution of the City Commission on April 16, 1980, which named each organization to be represented. In September 1982, the Commission formally recognized the Priority Board Structure as an "essential service," and in March 1986, the Community Development Block Grant (CDBG) Task Force reaffirmed the Priority Board in the same terms.

The Downtown Priority Board, coordinated by the Downtown Dayton Association, was established as a seventh Priority Board. Its director, Harry Imboden, had already been meeting with the Priority Board Chairpersons Council for several years. Subsequently, the Downtown Priority Board Steering Committee was formed.

B. Neighborhood Structures

1. Priority Board and Neighborhood Areas

Dayton is divided into seven Priority Board areas: six neighborhood Priority Boards and a downtown board represented by the Downtown Dayton Association and a Downtown Priority Board Steering Committee (representing residents of the downtown area). The downtown population is only 1,300, but the remaining Priority Board populations range from 15,000 to 72,000.

Each Priority Board area, except downtown, is further divided into a number of neighborhoods, from seven to seventeen within each board area. There were a total of seventy-three residential neighborhoods before a restructuring in 1987 that brought the number down to sixty-two. Population per neighborhood ranges widely, from a low of eleven people to a high of 10,300, although many of the smallest neighborhoods were absorbed into larger ones in the restructuring. The median neighborhood population, based upon the pre-1987 neighborhood lines, is 1,830 people.

2. Election to Priority Boards

Elections are held each year, separately from the municipal election (since 1975, they have been held during the month of July; in the downtown area they are held in April on a biannual basis). The elections are formally run by the Department of Human and Neighborhood Resources. They are structured according to an election plan submitted by the Priority Board each year, but these plans have remained fairly constant for a ten-year period.

Priority Boards have set terms of office of either two or three years, with correspondingly one-third to one-half of the seats open for election each year. The number of seats per board ranges from twenty-six to forty-five, for a total of 227 seats citywide. Four boards use a precinct basis for election, but with four different plans: with one seat per precinct, two per precinct, one per precinct plus five at-large, and one per two precincts plus ten representatives of neighborhood groups. Two others use "sub-neighborhoods" as the basis for election, and one of these adds ten at-large representatives. Finally, the seventh board, downtown, is composed solely of representatives of housing complexes and other organizations (including the local police precinct). All boards rely on the city for a mail ballot process, with the exception of organizational representatives who are chosen annually according to each organization's bylaws, and the downtown residential complexes, which send a representative from both the management and the tenants.

When a seat is contested, 30 to 50 percent of the time, mail ballots are sent out to every registered voter in that precinct. People have about one week to mail the ballot back in a pre-addressed, stamped envelope. Turnout in contested elections has ranged from 30 percent to 35 percent during the last five years, comparable to that of Dayton's municipal elections. In some precincts, turnout has reached 60 percent.

There is reimbursement for expenses from the city to each candidate, but only up to $35 per candidate. In order to get on the ballot, a candidate must be a registered voter and circulate a petition to obtain twenty-five signatures of registered voters in the area s/he represents.

3. Drawing Neighborhood and Priority Board Boundaries

The neighborhood and Priority Board boundaries were drawn by the planning department early in the development of the system. The Priority Board boundaries generally radiate out from the center of the city like the spokes of a wheel, most of the districts shaped like pie wedges, designed to include both lower-income people in the inner city and higher-income people near the city limits. One district, however, represents only the downtown, and another one represents almost exclusively the lowest-income neighborhoods in the city. Neighborhood boundaries tend to keep ethnic populations intact.

In 1986, under the Neighborhood Opportunities Plan, the director of the planning department redrew and renamed many neighborhoods. This seemed to be done in many places with surprisingly little input from neighborhood organizations. While most boundaries changed little, at least a quarter of the neighborhoods were substantially altered, often being combined with other neighborhoods or split into two pieces.

4. CP Administrative Funding

Funding from federal community development programs has always been important to the participation program in Dayton. The Community Development Block Grant program in particular has provided a substantial portion of the Priority Boards' budgets. In 1987, the total budget for the citizen participation system was $1.2 million, with 80 percent of this coming from CDBG and 20 percent from the city.

All of the participation funds in Dayton are directly administered by the Human and Neighborhood Resources Department, being divided between the central office and the six neighborhood Priority Board offices. Neighborhoods also receive substantial project funds and staff assistance through the Planning Department, especially the Neighborhood Opportunities Plan and the Neighborhood Initiative Program.

5. Priority Board Offices and Staff

As of 1987, the citizen participation system had twenty-eight staff members. Each of the six neighborhood Priority Boards typically has two or three professionals and one secretary who work out of the Priority Board office. These staff members are selected by the Priority Board itself from a short list that is provided by the central office after an initial screening process. Each staff member has a neighborhood-oriented performance contract which s/he must fulfill each year. The typical staff arrangement includes a coordinator, a community involvement advisor, and a person handling day-to-day complaints. At one point, the city's Personnel Board moved to place these staff under Civil Service, an action strongly opposed by the Priority Boards.

The staff occupies the middle ground between the city and the Priority Boards. One city administrator, reflecting a general view of city officials, noted that "most of the time the staff sides with the neighborhoods rather than the city." But they are generally seen by neighborhood people as city staff. For example, one Priority Board officer noted that "the city staff does a good job . . .

they get done what we (as Priority Board members) want them to get done."
Neighborhood leaders who are not on the Priority Board tend to view the staff
even more as an extension of the city rather than of the neighborhoods.

6. Priority Board Activities

The Priority Boards act both as "little city halls" for individual complaints
from residents and as focus points for neighborhood input on policy and programs of the city. They meet once or twice a month, and these meetings are
well publicized in advance through the newspapers. Some meetings have been
carried on public television.

While the boards do not have a formal role in the budget process, they all receive a copy of the proposed budget each year and have input at public hearings
on program strategy for the city. The city has met with the boards to receive
recommendations about essential services when budget cuts have become necessary. They are also frequent sounding boards for any new policy proposals
that a city agency is designing.

The largest role of the Priority Boards seems to be in the nitty-gritty of administration. They do a great deal to promote program changes in areas from
garbage collection to housing rehabilitation. Many neighborhoods present
their case first to the Priority Board in their area before taking it on to the appropriate city agency. Often the Board itself will take their case on for them.
The boards also play a major role in communicating issue positions to the public that the city feels are crucial to neighborhood vitality—from tax levies to
city employee resident requirements.

As one Priority Board member (who has since become a city official) noted:
"We are not just little neighborhood committees any more. We have real power
in the city. We drastically affected the school levy tax which was pushed by the
city [in 1982]. We supported this on the condition that a citizen participation
group be set up for the school system. The boards are strong enough that if they
would have said 'go to hell' [to the city], it is very likely that people would
have defeated the school levy."

C. Citywide Citizen Structures

1. Priority Board Chairpersons Council

One of the few citywide bodies that is fully representative of the Priority
Boards is the Chairpersons Council, which meets each week. This is much
more frequent than similar meetings in our other cities, and the Council seems
to have a status that is substantially greater than in our other cities as well.

While they have no formal powers on most issues, the Chairpersons Council frequently considers issues of citywide impact and often advocates specific positions before city agencies and occasionally before the City Council. The city manager is often a participant in these sessions.

2. *Capital Projects Task Force and Community Development Block Grant (CDBG) Task Force*

The CDBG Task Force determines all allocations for the program in the city. In theory, "more than half" of the members of this group represent citizens. There are sixteen members total. Each of the seven Priority Boards have one seat on the Task Force, as does the chair of the city planning board (considered a citizen member) and eight city officials. In practice, some Priority Board members feel that this group is generally dominated by the city officials present, typically staff members who can work on the issues full time and are paid for being at these meetings. Even those who have felt very happy with the process and its outcomes recognize an effective "city majority" in this body. Others, however, argue that there is usually an attempt to reach consensus, and there are not "too many cases of block voting."

The individual Priority Boards submit proposals for funding in the same manner that city agencies do. Out of nineteen proposals that were recommended for 1983, for example, seventeen came from Priority Boards or joint agency/Priority Board proposals. Out of 350 projects submitted to the Task Force in 1982, ninety-four were adopted. The city manager reviews these proposals, and they are finally approved by the city commission.

The CDBG Task Force meets each year from September to January (approximately). Ten factors are considered in rating each project. The CDBG task force always holds a hearing, and the City Commission holds two hearings for public comment on the city's CDBG proposed application.

A second group, the Capital Projects Task Force, is apparently much less formal, composed primarily of city staff. It reviews the remaining needs, after the CDBG Task Force is finished, and determines what resources can be found from sources other than CDBG to fund additional projects. Sometimes Priority Board projects ask for funds from other sources, but most deal with the CDBG process exclusively.

D. Outreach to Citizens

1. The *Dayton Update* is mailed to every household on a quarterly basis. It began in early 1982. Some Priority Board members feel that this is "not as

good" as the individual Priority Board newspapers had been before this time. The *Update* does have a reasonably comprehensive four-page section on the neighborhoods, however. It focuses on new programs available, on recreational opportunities, and on specific neighborhood news items such as grants, staff, events, and issue victories.

2. Neighborhood association mailings go out on an irregular basis. Most are one-page flyers describing recent events and announcing upcoming meetings. Many are mailed out of the Priority Board offices. Some slick neighborhood brochures are also produced by the planning department as a rotating promotion of specific neighborhoods.

3. Performance Reports on city agencies and Priority Boards are part of the regular "management by objectives" process in Dayton. They are particularly important in keeping staff aware of their responsibilities, and in monitoring the progress of each major project. These make their way, in summary form, to the final budget document each year, presented as explanations and justifications for specific items within the program budget. They are supplemented by evaluations from the population survey (see below). Except for their position in the annual budget, however, these reports do not seem to have any significant circulation to neighborhoods or the public at large.

4. The Priority Boards once had their own newspapers, but these were discontinued when the *Dayton Update* was started in 1982.

5. Unlike most cities of Dayton's size, the city manager's office initiates an annual population survey each year to find out how it is doing. This survey clearly provides detailed and timely feedback to the city about citizen interests, but city officials treat it as a routine process, and not as part of the participation system.

Usually contracted out to a local university, the survey asks dozens of questions about citizen satisfaction with specific city services, often focusing on one or two services each year. Highlights from this document are included in the annual budget document. In some cases specific management objectives are stated in terms of citizen response to this survey (for example, objective: improve citizen satisfaction with park maintenance by 3 percent in 1986; result: objective not obtained, satisfaction remained the same).

6. Surveys are occasionally conducted by individual neighborhoods and Priority Boards, often stimulated by some specific issue or proposal. Most are relatively informal, but some are very detailed and specific. A recent survey by the Deweese-Ridgecrest Civic Association, for example, asked for a priority rating by citizens on dozens of projects the group had undertaken. The results were successfully used both to shape organizational priorities and to persuade city officials to take action in the neighborhood.

E. Major Program Components

1. Priority Board Needs Statement

Neighborhood needs forms are distributed by the Priority Boards to the neighborhoods once a year. They are then returned to the Boards, which make up a Needs Statement to go to the city manager in August of that year. The Priority Boards document their needs through a number of means, including public surveys, hearings, open Priority Board meetings, committee and neighborhood group meetings, and administrative council complaint records. It is not clear how often the Priority Board staff actually writes up these proposals, and how many are written up directly by the neighborhoods.

These proposals are targeted to the appropriate city departments, which are supposed to address them in the following year's "work programs, objectives, and budgets." The presentation of the needs statements is apparently not done in any priority order. Included in each needs report is a list of capital project requests. These are in priority order within each Priority Board area. Since 1987, the Department of Human and Neighborhood Resources has produced a computerized listing of needs by neighborhood, and a computerized listing of departmental responses. It is too early yet to determine how helpful these will be in tracking the impact of the Priority Board requests.

2. Administrative Council

Established in 1975, the Administrative Council is a significant Dayton participation innovation. A Council meets monthly in each Priority Board area. In every Council session, a representative from each major city agency (and occasionally county and regional agencies) is available to take requests and respond to neighborhood problems and concerns. This process provides a regular opportunity for Priority Board members and other citizens to address specific service problems they may be having.

In practice, the Council conveys a sense that agencies are directly responsive to citizens. The physical setting makes it clear that it is the Priority Board, not the agency staff, who is running the process (a rare occurrence in most mixed groups of citizens and professionals). The agency representatives appear before the meetings not as experts who have the answers, but as staff ready to listen to Priority Board members. They do not usually come with prepared statements or reports, but are expected to respond to questions, complaints, or thank-yous from the Priority Board during the time in the meeting designated for that purpose. The issues tend to focus on individual cases that need to be resolved rather than on broad policy issues. And each case is followed up at the next meeting to ensure that appropriate action was taken. The process has by now become quite routine and seems to serve its purpose extremely well.

3. Neighborhood Opportunities Plan

This program was initiated by the planning department director in 1986. It had a one-million-dollar budget for each of the years 1986, 1987, and 1988, all from the general fund. In addition, the plan guides other departmental spending and over $6 million is sought from private sources, mostly for housing and business development. In 1987, it included thirty-two projects in ten project areas, covering such projects as:

- Boundary realignment and neighborhood gateways
- Tree maintenance; coordinated yard, street, and alley projects; and park and common space planning and relocation
- Comprehensive land use planning, demolition of structures, and vacant lot maintenance (with youth jobs project, below)
- Housing design and development (grants to Neighborhood Development Corporations), neighborhood marketing, and landlord training
- Business and institution development projects, loans, workshops
- Crime watches, security plans, street youth workers, and neighborhood mediation
- Neighborhood initiatives, welcoming, neighborhood artists, leadership training, and the festival of neighborhoods. Eight neighborhood groups received direct funding under the neighborhoods initiatives grants in 1986. Apparently, some $2 million has been given in such grants (NIP grants) since 1978.

4. Self-Help Neighborhood Grants Program

Self-Help grants are part of the Neighbor-to-Neighbor Program sponsored by the First National Bank and the Junior League (information for neighborhoods is provided at First National Bank offices). By the fall of 1983, six neighborhood organizations had received grants of up to $2,000 apiece. In 1986, ten neighborhoods received grants from Dayton Foundation money, apparently matched with city funds.

5. Neighborhood Conservation Program

This is a major effort run out of the Division of Inspectional Services by a former neighborhood activist. The goal is to use the housing enforcement code (plus residential zoning and environmental codes) to meet neighborhood objectives. Apparently, under its new director, the program has become very aggressive in bringing deteriorating housing up to code.

6. Leadership Training

The Neighborhood Leadership Institute is an annual program begun in early 1983 with twenty-five residents in the first program. It consists of a series of ten workshops scheduled in evenings and weekends on topics from city history and discussion of issues to effective neighborhood management and leadership roles. Residents get a certificate of completion for the course. In 1984, the program was coordinated by a Priority Board staff person. It is cosponsored by the Priority Boards and Bank One.

CityLinks, an annual weekend event sponsored by the University of Dayton and the Neighborhood Leadership Institute, is designed to cover major issues for making Dayton neighborhoods work.

7. Historic Districts

The six historic districts and the neighborhood organizations at their center have a special housing role in Dayton. They have made a clear difference in their neighborhoods, enabling extensive restoration and much less destruction of housing than has occurred in many parts of the city. Recent house tours given by the districts have attracted as many as 4,700 people. The districts seem to play a major role in helping to keep people interested in the inner city, and in preventing the depopulation that has been occurring in so many Dayton neighborhoods. The neighborhood organizations representing these districts often seem to have significantly more clout with many city agencies than other neighborhood associations in the city.

8. Dayton Education Council

A major task force operated during 1983 as part of a deal for Priority Board support of a school tax levy. The levy passed, the first one that did since 1971, and the schools developed a system of Community Education Councils as part of their agreement for increased participation. Half of each school council is composed of parents, and the other half is made up of community people, teachers, and administrators. Two representatives from each council go to regional meetings, one at each of the four high schools, and two representatives from each regional council go to the monthly meetings of the Dayton Education Council. The Dayton Education Council also includes representatives from other community organizations, ranging from the Dayton Area Realtors to the Dayton Urban League.

There has not been a close working relationship between the Council and the Board of Education, however. The Board has rarely sought advice, and the Council in its first years spent a great deal of time trying to figure out its role. It has worked with the superintendent of schools on several occasions on school reconstruction and improvement plans. But several council members felt that there remains a lack of support for the councils, from both the public and the school system. There has been very little communication between the councils and the Priority Boards.

9. Dayton Volunteers!

The Dayton Volunteers! program, begun in 1984, is now within the Neighborhood Affairs division. It attempts to coordinate and track volunteer placement for the city. In 1986, they logged over 77,544 hours of volunteer service to the city. A monthly volunteer newsletter now goes to all volunteers in the program, and items are placed in a monthly "Volunteering" column in the city's main daily newspaper. This office also runs the Dayton City Commission Community Service Awards for those providing exemplary volunteer services to the City of Dayton.

10. Other Projects and Events

One neighborhood development program provides summer jobs for youth. There is one supervisor for the program from each Priority Board area. The jobs focus primarily on neighborhood clean-up of alleys and vacant lots. Typically 100 to 150 youth participate each summer.

Numerous neighborhood events are encouraged and supported by the city. These include fairs, open houses, clean-up campaigns, and a variety of special celebrations. They have even included an annual "inner-city ball" each winter, sponsored by a coalition of neighborhood groups. Under one program to "market and promote the unique advantages of life and home ownership in the City of Dayton," the city reports that thirty-nine neighborhood events were conducted in 1986.

Special blue-ribbon commissions still exist in the city. In 1986, a commission on the police department issued its generally favorable report. Of seventeen members, it included only three Priority Board members, one NAACP member, and three churches. The rest were police-related groups, government, or business representatives.

F. Overall Perspective of the City on Participation

First and foremost, Dayton sees the Priority Board system as a two-way communications medium between citizens and the city. There is a clear sense that the system can help citizens influence and control government policies and actions. City administrators argue that participation in decision making is necessary "to encourage a sense of control and self-determination within the community. Citizens should participate directly in the shaping of governmental policies and other actions which affect their lives."

But the system is designed specifically for the city to reach citizens as well. Planning and strategy documents state that while Priority Boards have "provided government with representative indications of the needs and priorities of neighborhoods as well as assessments of City service effectiveness," it is also true that "City government in turn utilized Priority Boards to channel information to neighborhoods about government actions." Both ways of using the system are quite evident in the day-to-day operation of the system, and both directions of communication seem to have a substantial impact.

Two other features of the system are seen as central to its structure and operation: first, the ability of neighborhoods, which have the greatest stake, to enhance the "quality of neighborhood life" and "ensure the vitality of the area in which they live"; and second, the ability of neighborhoods to generate self-help projects beyond what the city itself can do. These concepts are the basis for the wide range of city efforts to promote strong neighborhood organizations and a strong sense of neighborhood identity. In many ways, the efforts of these neighborhood groups are seen as running parallel to, but not in lockstep with, the operations of the Priority Boards.

Portland Participation

A. Beginnings and Authorization
Born: February 1974
Place: In a city council ordinance creating the Office of Neighborhood Associations

The Portland citizen participation system grew out of the neighborhood associations that began forming in the mid-1950s to preserve the residential character of their neighborhoods. In the early 1970s, eight northeast neighborhoods had Model Cities Funds, five inner southeast organizations had Office of Economic Opportunity (OEO) funds, and the renewal agency had several field offices.

The specific pieces of the Portland system were developed in a two-year struggle to determine the best method of organizing these multiple programs, and of covering the whole city. The city-planning staff version was founded on a proposed system of District Planning Organizations (DPOs). By the beginning of 1973, all the political ingredients seemed to be in place to promote this approach: a DPO task force had met through 1972 to consider the proposals, budget authority for a Bureau of Neighborhood Organizations had been obtained by newly elected mayor Neil Goldschmidt, and Commissioner Mildred Schwab had developed a draft ordinance to implement the whole works. But at a meeting of 100 citizens to review this draft ordinance, major concerns were expressed that the DPOs would take power away from the neighborhood organizations. These concerns prevailed, even though a second tier of Neighborhood Planning Organizations had become part of the proposal by this time. A second draft, providing that DPOs would be established by neighborhood associations and have only the authority neighborhoods chose to delegate to them, fared no better.

Finally, in February 1974, the city council passed an enabling ordinance establishing the Office of Neighborhood Associations (ONA) , without any DPOs but with specific membership standards (open to residents, businesses, property owners, and nonprofits) and with formal council recognition of each neighborhood association. Even these two restrictions were dropped in the amended ordinance of November 1975.

The first year's budget (1973–74) was $105,000. By 1976–77, the budget was still only $187,000, passed in council by a three to two vote. In addition to these city general fund monies, federal money and local Portland Development Commission (PDC) money was also available, particularly in Southeast Portland.

At first all ONA contracts were directly with neighborhood associations. By 1976, coalitions had formed in only four areas:

- in Inner Northeast, a board existed as a successor to the Model Cities Board;
- in Inner Southeast, seven neighborhoods, successors to the OEO efforts, had formed a coalition;
- the larger Southeast, including the inner section, had developed a formal organization called Southeast Uplift, formed as a result of city council action directing Portland Development Commission funds to the southeast at the time Model Cities was established in the Northeast;
- and finally, seven smaller neighborhoods formed a coalition in North Portland.

Gradually, the "contracts" to oversee what have become the district offices were held by an ever-growing coalition of neighborhood groups. This finally led to the establishment of formal district boards (except, apparently, in the West/Northwest section). Only in April 1987 were formal written guidelines established for neighborhood groups, after a year-long process of negotiations between ONA and the groups.

B. Neighborhood Structures

1. Neighborhood Associations and District Boards

The basis of the Portland system are the neighborhood associations that exist in most of the city's ninety neighborhoods. These neighborhood associations send representatives to six District Coalition Boards (technically five; the sixth, in the West/Northwest, apparently has refused incorporation or recognition as a DCB). The downtown area, divided into two neighborhoods, has no District Coalition Board. And the Outer Northeast or Mid County area consists mainly of newly annexed areas and has yet to form a District Board. There are now from six to twenty-three neighborhoods within each of the District Coalitions. Population within these districts ranges from 19,000 to 143,000, while the populations of the individual neighborhoods range from 70 to 13,800. The median neighborhood population is 4,250.

A set of ONA Standards and Guidelines adopted in April 1987 is now the official standards that provide for recognition and support of a neighborhood association by the city. These guidelines include open membership requirements, prohibition of mandatory dues, and the same open-meeting requirements that governmental bodies must abide by. A heavy emphasis is placed on providing for and recording opposing views in any neighborhood process.

Membership in the neighborhood association must be open to all residents and property owners within the neighborhood boundaries. In addition, the associations can and do include others as official members (that is, businesses and nonprofits). They can also have boards and committees that meet more frequently than the general membership. These matters are governed by their individual bylaws.

2. Selection of Board Representatives and Neighborhood Officers

Elections for officers and representatives of neighborhood associations are governed entirely by the individual neighborhood bylaws. The District Coalition Boards are composed of delegates from each neighborhood association in their area, plus any special representatives (that is, of social service, business, or civic organizations) established in their bylaws. They must be incorporated and qualify as a nonprofit tax-exempt organization.

There are no other election requirements. Both the boards and the neighborhood associations are independent, self-governing bodies.

3. Drawing Neighborhood Boundaries

Each neighborhood determines its own boundaries and applies for recognition to the ONA based upon those boundaries. In the past, neighborhoods have been recognized with overlapping boundaries and even boundaries totally included within another neighborhood. The 1987 guidelines state that overlapping boundaries "should be discouraged" and assert that any boundary dispute will be resolved by the District Coalition Board, using the services of the neighborhood mediation center and surveys of area residents if necessary. The determination of boundaries is much more decentralized in Portland than in any of the other cities we have examined. There have been a few boundary disputes, but for the most part neighborhoods have boundaries with which each association feels comfortable.

4. CP Administrative Funding

The original funding for Portland's participation system was a mix of general funds and local and federal development funds. Most of the current budget comes from the general fund. The 1986–87 fiscal year budget for the participation system was 1.2 million dollars, exclusive of staff support for Budget Advisory Committees provided by the individual departments. Of this, over $1.1 million was from the general fund, while only $75,000 came from development funds of any kind. Approximately one-third of these funds are administered directly by the central Office of Neighborhood Associations, and the remaining two-thirds contracted out to the District Coalition Boards.

5. Offices and Staffing

There is now a central office, six district offices, two additional crime prevention offices (downtown and in North Portland), and a midcounty office (newly annexed areas).

Except for central office staff, all staff members are hired by, and are under the control of, the District Coalition Boards (or the equivalent in the West/Northwest). The Boards are under annual contract with the city to provide "citizen participation and crime prevention services." There are seven staff positions in the central office, and the District Coalition offices each have two or three staff, with the exception of the Southeast coalition (Southeast Uplift), which has nine. In addition, a mediation team of four people is located in the Northeast District office. Each district office develops its own set of written personnel policies and a work program, including procedures for annual performance reviews. They must have an affirmative action and equal opportunity policy that is approved by the city.

6. Neighborhood and District Activities

The District Coalition Boards typically meet once a month. Each district office has the responsibility to assist neighborhoods with whatever requests they may have—particularly in the area of producing newsletters for distribution to the households in the neighborhood. In addition, each district office has one full-time crime prevention coordinator whose major role is to assist in the organization of neighborhood crime watches and crime prevention efforts. Finally, each office is responsible for ensuring that neighborhood need reports are developed by the neighborhoods and the Board and transmitted to ONA. Beyond these basic functions, the district offices vary greatly in the work they do. Under the 1987 guidelines, they must file a semi-annual progress report and annual accomplishments report with the ONA.

The neighborhood associations are free to take on any issues in any way they choose. The only conditions on their activities are that they must be open to all residents and property owners, they must be nondiscriminatory and require no dues for participation, and any formal positions taken by neighborhood meetings must be recorded, along with attendance, the results of any votes, and a summary of dissenting views.

C. Citywide Citizen Structures

1. Budget Advisory Committees (BACs)

Four BACs were initiated by Mayor Goldschmidt in 1973. They were expanded over the next six years, and formally established by Commission ordinance in 1980. By 1987, twenty-one city bureaus had Budget Advisory Committees in place.

The membership of each BAC comes from many different sources, only one of which is the neighborhood association and district board system. They average a little over eight citizens per BAC. An attempt is made to have each of the six city districts represented on each committee, but there is no firm formula to guarantee such representation. All members of the BACs are appointed by the commissioner in charge. The stated goals of the process include helping to "produce a final budget that is responsive to the wishes and needs of the citizens of

Portland" and enabling citizens "to address policy questions of the City as a whole as well as recommend the policy direction of individual bureaus and departments."

The "Big-BAC" or Bureau Advisory Coordinating Committee (BACC) is composed of representatives from each of the BACs. In 1986, the BACC produced, in addition to the collection of BAC reports, a series of ten recommendations on issues such as long-range bureau planning, a volunteer program, a cost/benefit study of annexation, a plan to preserve the city's public works infrastructure, a crime-prevention plan, a citywide computer plan, and support for rebuilding fiscal reserves for the city.

Staff support for all the BACs comes primarily from the each bureau's staff, but ONA recruits members, coordinates the orientation process, and maintains BAC records and files.

D. Outreach to Citizens

1. Neighborhood Newsletters

The city contracts with each District Coalition Board to provide the funding equivalent for printing and mailing one neighborhood newsletter to each household in a neighborhood each year. The district offices provide technical assistance and secretarial services to produce these newsletters. The Southeast office has the capability to produce computer desktop-published newsletters and provides this service to some neighborhoods. If neighborhoods can find sources of in-kind services such as donated printing or volunteer door-to-door distribution, the city-provided funds can be stretched over more than one newsletter.

2. The ONA Newsletter

ONA produces a four-page newsletter ten times a year that goes to all neighborhood officers and individual citizens who have expressed an interest in receiving it. It does not attempt to cover all neighborhood events but provides a range of stories about recent successes.

3. District Coalition Newsletters

Four of the District Coalitions produce regular newsletters that cover the major issues facing the neighborhoods in its area. These newsletters often include statistical information, such as listings of reported crimes on a neighborhood-by-neighborhood basis. They also attempt to list most neighborhood meetings occurring each month in the Coalition area, which in the larger areas runs up to thirty to thirty-five events each month. The total coverage of households in the city by these newsletters can be quite high. In the Southeast district, for example, a total of 200,000 newsletters, between the district and its neighborhoods, were distributed in 1985–86.

4. District Surveys

Some boards conduct surveys of citizens in their district in conjunction with their neighborhood needs report. In the Northwest District, a neighborhood needs mailing is done each year to a mailing list of 1,000 households (out of approximately 11,000 in the district). Such surveys are not a regular process in most areas, however.

5. Citywide Population Survey

Since 1978, the city has conducted an annual population survey focusing on different issue areas each year. In the 1986 telephone survey of 1,200 residents (using a sample frame of 150 residents in each of five districts and downtown, plus two 150-person samples in two halves of the Southeast district), the 75 questions focused particularly on transportation and human resources, but covered many other service-related issues as well. The survey was completed under the auspices of the Office of Fiscal Administration.

E. Major Program Components

1. The Neighborhood Needs Process

This process now runs from September of each year to the following July. It begins with the distribution of forms by ONA to the District Coalition Boards and to the neighborhoods, accompanied by some training opportunities concerning the budget process. In October, ONA receives completed forms and transmits them to the appropriate bureau, which acknowledges its receipt to the person submitting the request. At this point a specific contact person in the bureau is assigned to handle the requests. By January, the bureau's response is sent to the neighborhood association and forwarded on to the commissioner in charge and to the mayor. The mayor makes his/her budget presentation in early April, and the final budget is passed by the Commission by June. By July, ONA sends out the final "neighborhood needs decision form."

Important components of this process include:

- As part of the initial needs identification, ONA provides a detailed checklist of potential problems, including about twenty-five questions and a listing of "need areas which traditionally have been a source of community concern."
- ONA "tracks" each need through a computer database organized by neighborhood and by bureau.
- The bureau response is sent to the originator of each individual needs request with the name and phone number of a bureau contact person. This includes a specific indication of whether the request was accepted, rejected, included in a budget package (with budget document number provided), or held for further review on a specific date.
- The bureau BAC reviews a listing of all bureau actions on neighborhood needs requests, as part of the bureau response phase in November and December of each year.
- The ONA "Neighborhood Needs Briefing Report" includes information on the process and timeline, sample forms, BAC contact lists, and a two-page description from several major bureaus on their services, priorities, example projects, and contact people.

2. Crime Prevention

Since crime has been the number-one issue in Portland during the past few years, crime prevention efforts are extensive. Full-time crime-prevention coordinators work out of the central ONA office and each district office. Their role is to help organize citizen crime prevention groups, many through neighborhood associations, and to help these groups gain access to the police and other city officials. The neighborhood watch is the central focus of this program.

3. Land Use and Comprehensive Neighborhood Plans

Land use planning in Oregon appears to be among the most elaborate in the country. Comprehensive plans in the state's major cities are mandated by state law. In Portland, many neighborhoods were involved in preparation of land use plans in the early 1970s, but only a handful actually seem to have produced full neighborhood-based comprehensive plans.

The strength of the system is that once such a plan is in place, state law makes it difficult to create variances and zoning changes that in many other states have made land use plans not worth the paper they are written on. Any individual or organization can challenge a land use decision that departs from the comprehensive plan, and is able to take the complaint to a state hearing officer. A result is that neighborhood organizations in Portland seem to have a very strong voice in any land use changes. The Fred Meyer case, at one extreme, pitted one of the biggest local corporations against several neighborhoods. In this case, the neighborhoods lost the administrative battle but took the issue to the state Supreme Court.

4. Self-Help Grants from the Housing and Community Development Department

This program only operates in specifically designated HCD (Housing and Community Development) neighborhoods. Most of the money for these grants comes from the federal Community Development Block Grant Program. Contrary to other cities in our study, the CDBG process seems to be almost totally independent from the participation system, and not very responsive to it. These CDBG grants are administered by an autonomous body, the Portland Development Commission. Throughout the history of the Portland system, this HCD process and the participation process seem to have run on parallel tracks, with little connection except within specific neighborhood associations that received support both through HCD and ONA.

5. Leadership Training and Neighborhood Small Grants Program

For several years, one-day leadership training conferences were provided by the Southeast District Coalition Board (Southeast Uplift) for the whole city. The conference was designed to develop ways for neighborhoods to be more effective in organizing and presenting their issues to city hall. There were 130 participants in 1985.

This program is funded by the Neighborhood Grant Program of the Oregon Community Foundation. Individual neighborhood associations have also received grants from this foundation program. The Southeast board runs several other training and issues forums each year, focusing on topics such as housing, crime, and drugs.

6. Neighborhood Technical Assistance Program

Another major neighborhood training organization is the Center for Urban Education. Receiving significant church-based and foundation funding, the Center has a dozen programs focused on the nitty-gritty of neighborhood organization development, from computer-assisted newsletters to effective volunteer programs and the use of a technical assistance resource bank.

7. Central City Plan

This three-year effort to redesign the downtown area of Portland was developed by a special task force created by one of the city commissioners to bypass both the Portland Development Commission and the Planning Department (the latter being under the control of a mayor who, at the time, was relatively unsympathetic to citizen participation).

The first year of the plan saw an enormous participation effort, eliciting the responses of over 10,000 citizens. Outreach efforts included special festivals, a mobile information van, self-operated computer programs to survey citizen attitudes, and a wide range of creative participation initiatives.

The budget and timetable for the process were overrun, however, and as the program was transferred to a new commissioner, major cutbacks were made and most of the participation component disappeared. The whole process operated relatively independently of the neighborhood associations, although several of the Inner Southeast neighborhoods were specifically involved.

8. Neighborhood Information and Neighborhood Organizing Materials

ONA was also designated manager of the city's information and referral center. The program's offices were moved in 1987 to occupy nearly half of the first floor of city hall in order to be more visible. The effect of this move on the operation of the office has yet to be seen.

In addition to the documents it has always produced to suggest how to organize a neighborhood association and how to work with the Budget Advisory Committees or the neighborhood needs process, ONA is now responsible for basic information for citizens about all local governmental functions. To some extent they share this function with the independently elected city auditor's office (which functions much like a city clerk in other cities) across the corridor in city hall.

ONA is also responsible for maintaining a calendar of all neighborhood meetings and events and a list of all neighborhood contacts, updated twice a month. These resources supplement those of the individual district offices, which also make available such information for their own areas.

9. Neighborhood Mediation Center

Located in the Inner Northeast District office, this center provides professional mediators and trains volunteer mediators to help resolve individual neighbor-to-neighbor problems before the courts get involved. They also mediate between businesses, neighborhood associations, nonprofit organizations, and the Housing Authority.

10. Neighborhood Commercial Districts

Formal organizations within specific commercial districts of the city were increasing in number and visibility in 1986. An Alliance of Portland Neighborhood Business Associations has been formed to represent their interests. In many ways, they have been inspired by the neighborhood associations, but they also reflect a sense that the interests of local business establishments are not necessarily well represented by the neighborhood associations or district boards. In most situations, however, the commercial associations and neighborhood associations seem to have worked well together to resolve specific issues in the community.

11. Other Projects and Events

The second week of May is "Neighborhood Recognition Week." It involves day and evening workshops with staff from six major city bureaus that affect neighborhood life, presentations and small group discussions between neighborhood leaders and city council members, and individual and organizational recognition through the Mayor's Spirit of Portland Awards.

The Neighborfair is held in Waterfront Park, the downtown area bordering the Willamette River that was reclaimed from an old arterial highway. Sponsored by KGW, a local radio station, this fair has drawn as many as 250,000 people from the city and nearby suburbs. Individual neighborhood associations are able to have booths at the event, recruit new members, and demonstrate the results of specific projects they have undertaken.

F. Overall Perspective of the City on Participation

Portland seems to be a good example of a city in which reluctant officials were often brought along by citizens into a growing participation system. The focus of the system is clearly on the individual neighborhood associations and their ability to make things happen. Unlike St. Paul, Dayton, or Birmingham, where the neighborhood-level groups are frequently created by the city, a large proportion of Portland's neighborhood associations have a history of autonomy from city hall. They demonstrated their power in the late 1960s and early 1970s by stopping or drastically modifying a number of projects, including redevelopment efforts (such as the Albina slum clearance) and major highway projects (such as the Mt. Hood Freeway). The recognition of these neighborhood associations by city hall was born out of this activism. From the beginning of ONA, the individual neighborhoods have fought any sign of structure or control by city hall on their own activities—only after several years were district offices accepted, and only after fourteen years would neighborhoods accept written guidelines covering their operation.

Several commissioners, which have independent administrative powers in Portland's commission form of government, and at least one mayor have not been supportive of the ONA operation. Yet substantial allocation of the city's general funds has been maintained throughout the history of the participation system. In spite of other budget cutbacks in many other agencies, the ONA funding seems to have been increasing every year.

With this history, the goals of ONA are generally stated in terms of considering and acting upon citizen needs. Participation in decision making is a major factor in the design of nearly every new program in the city. Officials frequently make clear that the ONA system itself is only part of participation in the city—no individual or group is to be discouraged from participating "directly in the decision-making process of the City Council or any City Agency." Citizen activists also express a strong feeling that each neighborhood has a style all its own, a definite sense of values, and an opportunity to take any of a multitude of participation paths to city hall. In some ways, there may be an underlying fear that making any one participation route too powerful may allow one interest or another to gain too much influence. In any event, the system strives for a balanced approach to participation rather than dependence upon any one agency or structure.

St. Paul Participation

A. Beginnings and Authorization

Born: October 9, 1975

Place: In five resolutions of the City Council defining citizen participation, authorizing the mayor to set up participation councils where they did not yet exist, and allocating funds for the participation system.

1967

A City Planning Board map dated August 1967 shows the city divided into Planning Area Units composed of approximately eighteen "communities" and fifty "neighborhoods."

1972

Mayor Lawrence Cohen formed a Committee on Citizen Participation in June 1972, fulfilling his election campaign promise to examine "in detail" the question of "how to create the best possible structure and process of participation of citizens in the affairs of Saint Paul government." His invitation letter to committee participants noted the evident need for citizen participation at all levels of government to restore citizen trust, and indicated that, at the time, "citizens often feel that their government is a hostile institution which is actively working against them."

The mayor's stated purpose in establishing the participation committee was to enable "reconsideration of the relation of community groups to city government." Apparently a number of strong citizen groups and community councils had existed for some time in St. Paul and were to be important in any new system. Cohen envisioned community council elections by that November.

1973

In a March 27, 1973, resolution, the City Council unanimously approves the appointments of the twelve committee members, who apparently had already been meeting for nine months. Two more members were approved by Council resolution on July 17. Mayor Cohen and Councilwoman Rosalie Butler were among the committee members. Three others represented a group called the Association of Saint Paul Communities. The committee distributed a "Community Council Questionnaire" to groups and individuals and held five public hearings.

The final report of the committee, "Making Democracy Work," was completed on September 26, 1973. It recommended a participation system very similar in design and spirit to the one currently in place in St. Paul. Four committee members issued a brief minority report recommending that the councils have final authority over zoning and public improvements in their areas, and that the city's Planning Commission be restructured to represent these councils directly. Apparently both majority and minority proposals were defeated.

1975

Mayor Cohen and two councilpersons (Hozza and Sylvester) try again to establish a citizen participation system in the city. A League of Women Voters report notes: "The catalyst for the attempt was the Community Development program which specified that federal funds could be used for citizen participation." Approximately $267,000 was put into a "contingency fund" for citizen participation. City officials took the lead, proposed a system of seven or eight participation districts, and convened a forum on January 28, 1975. Over 450 people attended. The League reports, "It was quickly evident that many felt resentment toward city government." This was the first of several weekly meetings of the Citizen Participation Forum, which then continued to operate, through task forces and general meetings, until at least the fall of 1975.

On July 22, 1975, the City Council adopted a resolution that accepted proposals from the Forum, including a structure of seventeen districts and an "early warning communications system" for citizens, and called for a forty-five to sixty day "cooling off period" before taking further action. The proposed resolution presented to the Council in July by the Forum was not adopted. The major points of disagreement apparently centered on a uniform council structure (especially its relation to existing citizen groups), and on the formal power of the district council in planning and development issues. On October 9, the Council passed resolutions defining participation "as a process, not a structure," authorizing the mayor to "create or improve the participation process" in each district when district planning teams or neighborhood groups felt the district was ready, and providing $50,000 for these purposes to the mayor while continuing $10,500 per month to the "neighborhood development planning areas" which had been created under earlier federally funded projects. Representatives of the Forum formally stated that they did not support the City Council resolution but nevertheless disbanded the Forum at this point. Councilman Sylvester apparently wrote the final resolutions that passed the council. His report of September 30, 1975, asserted the following:

- each council should determine its own structure involving new or existing groups,
- the city and each council should develop an agreed work plan (avoiding use of the term "contract"), and
- recognition of each new council should follow a ten-point plan involving an inventory of existing community groups, definition of boundaries, creation of bylaws, and final approval by the City Council.

Sylvester's final proposals became the basis for the participation system still in place today in St. Paul.

B. Neighborhood Structures

1. District Councils

The seventeen District Councils that completely cover the city of St. Paul are by far the strongest, most visible part of the system. As in all the cities we have examined, the downtown district is much less developed than the rest. The population of the council areas ranges from 7,000 to 26,000, except for the downtown area, which includes 3,300 residents. The median district population is 15,800.

Each council is a separately incorporated nonprofit organization, and several have or are applying for 501.c3 tax-exempt status. While each District Council has been formally recognized by the City Council, and receives funds from the city, each remains a relatively self-governing body in all other ways. Their structure, elections, relationship to other citizen organizations, officers, committees, staff, and office location and functions are all determined solely by the council itself, through its formal bylaws. Each organization is free to raise additional funds from any source open to a nonprofit organization. Only two visible city restrictions exist: the councils must be nonpartisan, and the money from the city must be used for its stated purposes—to hire a community organizer, for example, rather than a secretary.

2. Elections

The method of selection of each council is determined by each organization's bylaws:

- Fifteen of the districts elect the council at annual meetings, two at polls in a separate election.
- Seven are all at-large, eight have elections by subdistricts, two others have mixed representation systems.
- Nine have specific positions for representatives of neighborhood or business groups, in addition to the council members elected by the general membership
- The size of the council ranges from six to thirty-one members, with most having fifteen to twenty.
- Average turnout at annual meetings ranges from thirty to two hundred people.

3. Drawing Neighborhood Boundaries

Boundaries for the districts were largely determined by the original citizen participation committee and forum. It was widely noted in the reports of these committees that citizens did not trust the city to come up with a set of boundaries. According to the ten-point recognition plan, the citizen groups within a proposed district "should first make every effort to reach agreement among themselves on the boundaries. If there is a dispute, citizen groups should be given a maximum of forty-five days to resolve the matter. Any disputes are to be finally resolved by the City Planning Department."

Apparently most boundaries were settled by consensus, in large part follow-ing the lines of the 1967 community map of the Planning Department. Only in District 13 was a permanent lack of consensus obtained, resulting in a split of the district between three different organizations. Boundaries have occasion-ally been changed, most recently with a slight restructuring between Districts 9 and 15 in southwest St. Paul.

4. CP Administrative Funding

In contrast to the structures in our other cities, the St. Paul participation system has very little centralized administration. All the money allocated to the partic-ipation system goes directly to the district councils, with the exception of funds for the salary and expenses of the citywide participation coordinator, which are paid from the Planning and Economic Development Department budget. In 1987–88, the total budget allocated by the city to the District Councils was $485,652. The sources of these allocations are the Community Development Block Grant for the eleven districts eligible for CDBG ($371,386), and general funds for the remaining six districts ($113,266). This breaks down to between $20,000 and $36,000 for each district.

Furthermore, city funds are only part of the financial picture in St. Paul. A substantial amount of United Way funds are allocated to community centers in eight of these districts (up to $480,000 in one district), and these centers are often a hub for the District Council activities. Grants from the McKnight Foun-dation Neighborhood Self-Help Initiatives Program (MnSHIP) have in some years increased the operating budget of certain councils by as much as 50 per-cent. For the 1987–88 fiscal year, over $423,000 came into the councils from noncity, non–United Way sources, in addition to funds for a half-million-dollar block nurse program being administered by one District Council. These addi-tional funds are used by each District Council entirely at their own discretion without any city oversight.

The city allocation was under heavy pressure in 1988 because of cutbacks in the city's CDBG funds from the federal government.

5. Offices and Staffing

Each district has its own office and staff, paid for out of its own operating bud-get. The staff are selected directly by the District Council, with less role for the city than in any of the other participation systems we examined. Staff numbers range from one to over three, with a typical staff being a full-time person with a half-time assistant, or two part-time people. The equivalent of at least thirty-two full-time staff people worked in the District Councils in 1988.

Staff salaries are more in line with citizen-group organizers ($12,000 to $22,000) than with city employees. This was a cause for serious complaint in the late 1980s. Attempts were made to form a union of sorts among the staff to lobby for higher salaries and higher total grants from the city.

The city had one staff person who served as Citizen Participation Coordinator. S/he works officially in the Planning and Economic Development Department but in practice is largely independent.

6. Neighborhood Activities

A great deal of the activity of each Council seems to revolve around the large number of requests for response that come from the city. Several staff members complained that these requests kept them too busy to do other tasks pressing upon their district. Since there appears to be no penalty for ignoring the re quests, except perhaps reduced influence with the city in certain areas, this problem seems to be within the control of appropriate priority setting in District Council itself.

While each Council does set very different priorities for itself, all have a significant focus on land use issues. This may include requests for zoning variances by developers, siting for single-resident-occupancy housing sought by the city, street and sewer reconstruction, environmental impact questions, or providing adequate off-street parking. In all of these areas, major issues have arisen and been resolved during the past few years with heavy involvement of the District Councils.

Beyond some of the core land use issues, each Council is involved in a wide range of other activities. These projects include crime watches, recycling, hazardous waste and pollution control, neighborhood clean-ups, drainage projects, festivals, arts projects, community gardens and composting, traffic control, park development, employment training, antipornography campaigns, tree planting, and energy audits. Another major consequence of St. Paul's district orientation has been the construction of large community centers in many of the District Council areas during the last fifteen years (see description below).

C. Citywide Citizen Structures

1. Long-Range Capital Improvement Budget Committee (CIB)

One of the few cases of major citywide impact for the participation systems we have seen is represented by the CIB Committee in St. Paul. This committee is part of a Unified Capital Improvement Program and Budget Process, which deals with all capital funds available to the city during a two-year period—including federal and state grants and local bond revenues.

There are eighteen members of the committee: seventeen are nominated by the Districts and approved by the mayor and City Council, the eighteenth is appointed by the mayor and approved by the Council. In addition, three task forces that do the first stage of project evaluation (Community Facilities, Streets and Utilities, Residential and Economic Development) are directly appointed by the District Councils with one representative and one alternate from each Council on each task force, no city approval being required. Members of the overall CIB committee serve as officers for each task force. Overall, then, as many as 120 citizens have a direct role in determining the capital budget for the city of St. Paul.

Staff for the committee is provided by the mayor's budget office, supported by planning department personnel. Proposals for the next biennial budget are submitted to the CIB by city departments, the District Councils, and individual citizens, and are assigned to the appropriate task force. Each member of each task force rates all proposals assigned to that task force using an elaborate point system. The ratings of all task force members are combined and each project is listed in order of its combined score. The task force then goes over each project, in rank order, and votes upon a recommended funding amount. During this evaluation period, bus tours to the affected areas and meetings with the District Councils in the area are often arranged.

The recommendations of each task force go to the full CIB committee, where final changes can be made. They then go to the mayor and the City Council. The system is unusual in the weight it gives to district representatives instead of city staff. Even in the initial proposal submission, we are told that the districts often have the advantage, with city departments sometimes seeking out district co-sponsorship of proposals before they are submitted. The mayor and City Council apparently change very little in the typical capital budget after the CIB recommendations are made. We are told that 70 to 80 percent of the projects finally funded were initiated by the districts.

Some projects are "directly implemented" by the District Council. This apparently means that the District Council receives funds to do the job. Examples include a crime prevention manual, a premises survey, and a neighborhood housing services program.

D. Outreach to Citizens

1. Council Meetings and Meeting Notification

All District Councils meet at least once a month, with most having separate executive committee and issue committee meetings each month as well. Each district uses a different means to reach residents of the district. Mailing and literature drops are common, with at least one-third of the districts mailing to all households on a quarterly basis or more frequently. Almost all do door-to-door distribution of flyers in several block areas affected by specific issues; for some districts this is done on practically a weekly basis. The amount of outreach in most districts compares favorably with many of the best community groups we have seen throughout the country.

2. District Newspapers

More than twelve of the districts are served by neighborhood newspapers. Most are published monthly, a few bimonthly or biweekly. These tend to be run by independent citizen groups with lots of volunteer labor. A few are run by the District Council itself. These newspapers provide good coverage for the district, tending to have a calendar and several articles each month on issues related to the councils. Most are distributed to every household in the district. These papers are a source of great pride to the districts and those without active papers usually place a high priority on finding a way to develop one.

3. Block Clubs

Several of the districts have placed a high priority on the development of block clubs within the district, usually as part of a crime watch program. Several districts have received MnSHIP grants to fund block club organizers, and a few claim to have a block captain on every block in the district. (District 14 boasts 350 block clubs, and districts 12 and 16 have organized 120 each). These block clubs typically serve as communication links to the residents, in addition to their crime-watch activities. Block club captains are often responsible for distribution of issue flyers and meeting notices to all residents. Maintenance is difficult: a periodic task for many District Councils is rejuvenation of the system of block clubs in their area.

E. Major Program Components

1. Early Notification System (ENS)

This system was formally detailed in an eight-page ordinance enacted in August 1979. Its stated purpose is "to provide TIMELY information to community organizations regarding the City's various activities that are being considered, proposed, planned or implemented. Further, the system facilitates feedback to the City regarding the neighborhoods' response and position."

The ENS system consists of a two-part mailing list (by district and citywide) and a policy for using and maintaining the list. Included on the list are the community organizers in each district, two District Council members, two members from each citizen organization in the city, and neighborhood newspapers. The system requires that each ENS communication designate the districts affected and the contact person in the sending agency. A log of all such mailings is required, with quarterly reporting to the citizen participation coordinator.

All major agencies must send meeting notices and agendas to the ENS mailing list, and other committees and commissions may be required to do so if a request is made by citizen organizations or the coordinator. One provision states that any district may request that a controversial issue be held over until the next regularly scheduled meeting. Tavern and liquor licenses require a forty-five-day notice through the ENS system, as do "development ads, street vacations, special assessments, and any public policies affecting neighborhoods." Quarterly notices of public lands available for redevelopment are also part of the ENS system. Detailed requirements are given for notices involving rezoning, "determination of similar use," conditional uses and variances, "40-acre study," and building condemnations and demolitions.

In general, the ordinance adopts the tone and substance of the participation system itself. For example, the ordinance exhorts city officials to "emphasize the positive aspects of what City government is proposing. In every case possible, do more than simply notify: explain reasons behind a project, activity, or change." The citizen participation coordinator is the ENS manager, with responsibilities that extend to maintaining the ENS mailing list, establishing a central log of mailings, and training city staff on how to use the system.

2. District Plans

In the late seventies, most districts worked on land use plans for their area. Some are undergoing revision at this time. Staff from the Planning and Economic Development Department have spent a great deal of time assisting in the formation of these plans. But it is unclear how effective these have been for managing growth and development in the districts. We did not frequently hear them referred to by the District Council leaders. A 1970s planning department report notes that this planning process "brought lots of city staff out to neighborhood meetings" and was designed to be tied into the capital budgeting process.

3. City Planning Staff support

A striking feature in St. Paul is the degree to which the staff of the Planning and Economic Development Department (PED) are neighborhood-oriented. There seems to be a very high degree of communication between PED staff and the District Council staff. Most project plans and proposals, except those for the downtown area, seem to be cleared through the appropriate District Councils before staff take them to the Planning Commission or the City Council. These include capital improvement projects to be proposed to the Capital Improvement Budget Committee. Several divisions of the planning department specifically target neighborhoods as the basis for their operations.

4. Community Centers

At least eight of the districts have major community centers of their own. These facilities typically house up to a dozen nonprofit organizations and provide a focus for community meetings and recreational opportunities in the district. Apparently much of the construction cost for these buildings originally came out of the CDBG and CIB process. Since their construction, however, maintenance and staffing for the buildings has sometimes been a problem. The United Way covers a substantial share of this cost, in two districts nearly two-thirds (or over $350,000 per year). A number of current issues for the District Councils revolve around ways to find funds for continued maintenance and staffing of these facilities.

5. Neighborhood Partnership Program

A major development program of the city, the Neighborhood Partnership Program (NPP), is designed to fund small business ventures created by individual entrepreneurs. Over the course of six years (1980–86), NPP has awarded over $4 million to 42 projects, with a private funding match of over $20 million. These have ranged from commercial- and residential-area revitalization programs to crime watch, human service, and community art projects. District Councils have occasionally taken advantage of these programs through the development of applications of their own.

6. Advisory Boards

There are at least thirty citizen advisory boards to government agencies in St. Paul. Most receive appointments by the mayor or the City Council. Two special types of advisory boards affecting neighborhoods are the Mayor's Rehabilitation Advisory Committee and six Identified Treatment Area (ITA) committees. The ITA committees provided oversight for several major development-oriented projects located in half a dozen districts in the 1979–83 period.

7. Citizen Monitoring and Evaluation Process

The St. Paul Citizen Monitoring and Evaluation Process, which began in 1978, is focused on the CDBG program but includes all aspects of the unified capital budget process. It includes quarterly and annual status reports sent to "interested citizens," evaluation sessions held annually by city staff at District Council meetings in districts that receive CDBG funds, and an annual citywide Performance Hearing. With the major impact of the CIB process, however, this monitoring operation seems to play a smaller role than in many other cities.

8. District Council Leadership and Board Development

Several of the boards have received grants, primarily from the McKnight Foundation's MnSHIP program, to help with board training. Ron Hick, an outspoken advocate of neighborhood empowerment and frequently a critic of the District Council system, has been one of the trainers in this program. The city itself seems to take a minimal role in this process.

9. Neighborhood Information

The Planning and Economic Development Department is the source of most neighborhood information in the city. It produced the book *St. Paul Today* and the "St. Paul Tomorrow" study, both extensive sources of comparative information by neighborhoods. The Citizen Participation Coordinator also provides a great deal of information about the Districts and is the chief troubleshooter for the whole operation.

In addition, an Office of Information and Complaint reports to the City Council. Their primary role is to direct citizens to the right government agency to take care of their problems. This office has no direct ties to the District Council system, but the office does work with community organizers in the districts when appropriate questions or requests come in from citizens.

The primary contact point for citizens to receive information about their neighborhood in St. Paul is their local District Council. Almost all information that goes out from the city which relates to the participation system in any way includes the names, address, and phone number of all seventeen District Council offices and community organizers.

10. Other Projects and Events

- Altogether, the McKnight Foundation's Neighborhood Self-Help Initiative Program has more than $5 million available for Minneapolis and St. Paul neighborhoods during the next ten years.
- The city also has had a Neighborhood Business Revitalization Program since 1982.
- Mayor Latimer asked the districts to submit priorities for a Better Neighborhood Program in 1986.

- The city has a number of citizen-administrator task forces to work on specific problems for a limited time. One recent task force, on Community Residential Facilities, proposed changes in state law and city ordinances to better distribute halfway houses and the like throughout the city. Six of the ten non-Planning Commission members of the task force were from District Councils. Other recent task forces have focused on dangerous traffic patterns on Shepard Road, Snelling-University neighborhood design, college zoning, and parking in Victoria Crossing.
- The Riverfront Initiative is a long-range planning project for St. Paul's riverfront areas. In addition to the usual planning operations, and attention-gathering events such as arts projects and the Mississippi Peace Cruise, a small grants program is offering funds for citizens and groups to develop events on or about the riverfront.

F. Overall Perspective of the City on Participation

St. Paul has a history of independent neighborhood groups and a reputation among its citizens for citizen participation. Born in an era of city versus citizen group confrontation, the theme of the participation system lies in people working together to build better neighborhoods, and in citizens having a direct role in the city's decision-making process. Land use planning and control and communication with citizens are seen as central roles for the district councils.

The participation structure has gradually grown into one of the most coherent and comprehensive of any city we have seen. While originally proclaiming that participation is process, not structure—because the city and citizen groups could not obtain agreement on the complete structure—clearly defined structure has become a mainstay of the St. Paul system. From the CIB system to the District Councils themselves, the structure that has developed gives every appearance of being there to stay. Almost all participation opportunities offered by the city are funneled through the council system. Because councils were given such a substantial role, other citizen groups came to feel that there was an overwhelming advantage in becoming part of the council system. And so they did. The result may be somewhat cooptive of independent citizen action, but the variety that does exist is striking: each district has its own style and mode of operation, which grew out of its original citizen group beginnings.

A substantial advantage to the St. Paul system is that each neighborhood of 7,000 to 26,000 people is able to have its own office and at least one full-time staff person. The grant from the city seems to come with very few strings attached. The main "string" is the dependency the group develops on this city money. On the other hand, since each neighborhood has staff, each neighborhood has a substantial level of activity. Unlike every other city we looked at, no part of St. Paul suffers from a complete lack of citizen organization.

Appendix C

Components of the Core, Outreach, and Involvement Measures Used in Creating the Neighborhood Strength Index

Core Activity

Basic Index

0 No activity	No meetings and no officers
1 Sporadic activity	Meets occasionally (1 to 8 times in to 2 years)
2 Low to moderate activity	Meets 9 to 19 times in 2 years
3 Consistent, regular activity	Meets 20 to 24 times in 2 years
4 High activity	Meets 25 to 36 times in 2 years
5 Exceptional activity	Meets 37 times or more in 2 years

Other indicators of core activity will increase or decrease rating by one or two levels as follows:

ALL CITIES: BUDGET

Per-capita budget less than $.15	No addition
Per-capita budget $.15 up to $1.00	Add one level in core
Per-capita budget $1.00 or more	Add two levels in core

DAYTON: PRIORITY BOARD REPRESENTATIVES

Unusually high level of representation (2 or more organizational representatives or an organizational representative plus 5 or more precinct representatives)	Add one level in core activity

PORTLAND: ELECTIONS, NEEDS, AND DISTRICT COALITION REPRESENTATIVES

If any two elements are less than normal (i.e., no needs, no representative, or only one election in two years)	Subtract one level in core

BIRMINGHAM: ACTIVITY OF OFFICERS, INCORPORATION, ALLOCATION

If officers have typical activity, no incorporation, and rare use of allocation	Subtract one level in core
If officers are particularly active and group is incorporated or always use allocation	Add one level in core

ST. PAUL: STAFFING AND SPECIAL FUNDRAISING

If per capita budget is $1.00 or more
but:

• If staff is less than 1.5 per district	Subtract one level
• If per capita budget raised by group is >$1.00, and staff is 2.0 or more per district	Add one level

Outreach

Basic Index

$$\frac{\text{Frequency of newsletter production} \times \text{Distribution}}{\text{total number of households in district}}$$

plus

$$\text{Special Projects rating (primarily frequency)}$$

Other indicators of outreach will increase rating by one or two levels as follows:

PORTLAND:

For neighborhoods that occasionally distribute materials to every household, in addition to a regular newsletter	Add frequency of special distributions

BIRMINGHAM:

For neighborhoods that put an unusual effort into their newsletter, up to and including publishing themselves (instead of simply submitting material to the city)	Add one outreach level
For neighborhoods that are only rated by Community Resource Officers as "somewhat" active with their newsletter	Subtract one outreach level

For neighborhoods that are rated by Community Resource Officer as "inactive" on newsletter

Subtract two outreach levels

ST. PAUL:
For neighborhoods that do extensive sign posting, flyering in addition to newsletter, or major phone outreach

Add one outreach level

Involvement

Basic Index

$$\frac{\text{Regular meeting attendance} \times (200 \text{ norm. factor})}{\text{population}}$$

$$+ \frac{\text{special event attendance} \times (5 \text{ norm. factor})}{\text{population}}$$

Other indicators of participation will increase rating by one or two levels as follows:

DAYTON:
For neighborhoods that have special event volunteers;

$$\frac{\text{Add number of event volunteers} \times (30 \text{ norm. factor})}{\text{population}}$$

BIRMINGHAM:
For blockwatch activity
 very active
 moderately active

Add one level
Add .5 level

ST. PAUL:
For blockwatch activity

$$\frac{\text{Add activity}}{4}$$

For annual meeting attendance

$$\frac{\text{Add attendance} \times (100 \text{ norm. factor})}{\text{population}}$$

Data Sources

BIRMINGHAM: Phone and in-person interviews with community resource officers
DAYTON: Phone interviews with Priority Board staff
PORTLAND: In-person interviews with District Coalition Board staff
ST. PAUL: Phone interviews with District Council staff

Data Items for All Cities

	Value Range	Variable Name
1. Neighborhood population (from 1980 census)	# people	POPULATION
2. Does organization have current officers?	y or n	OFFICERS
3. Has organization had regular elections for officers during the last two years?	y or n	ELECTIONS
4. Number of regular meetings in last two years	0 to 48	REG_MEET
5. Number of people attending regular meeting (avg)	# people	REG_ATTEND
6. Number/Rating of Special projects in last two yrs.	0 to 5	SPEC_PROJ
7. Number of people attending special events (sum)	# people	SPEC_ATTEND
8. Frequency of newsletter production in two years	0 to 48	NEWSFREQ
9. Number of households receiving newsletter (avg)	# households	NEWSDIST
10. Frequency of materials distrib. to all hsehlds.	0 to 24	NEWSALL
11. Annual budget	$ amount	BUDGET

Additional Data Items

Birmingham	Value Range	Variable Name
12. Degree of crimewatch block club organization	1 to 3	BLOCKWATCH
1 = none active (default)		
2 = some are active, and some are not		
3 = nearly all blocks have block watch		
13. Neighborhood has nonprofit corporation? (n is default)	y or n	INCORP
14. Neighborhood usually spends all of its allocation from the city each year	1 to 4	ALLOC
1 = Never spends funds		
2 = Spends some funds (default)		
3 = Spends most of allocation		
4 = Spends all of allocation each year		
For officers item (2), Birmingham has a scale:	1, 2, 3	OFFICERS
1 = officers not active		
2 = officers somewhat active (default)		
3 = officers very active		
For NEWSALL, Birmingham has a scale:	1 to 4	NEWSALL
1 = Not active, CRO must call		

2 = Somewhat active, NA calls CRO
3 = Very active with newsletter
4 = NA works and publishes own newsletter

The BUDGET item in Birmingham represents the amount raised by the neighborhood association only; it does not include the city allocation.

The SPEC_PROJ and SPEC_ATTND items for Birmingham were each derived from the sum of three event items: "issue decision meetings" (SPEC1), "rallies/work projects" (SPEC2), and "festivals and parties" (SPEC3). The attendance in each category appears in the variables SPEC1A, SPEC2A, and SPEC3A respectively. SPEC_PROJ = round((SPEC1 + SPEC2 + SPEC3)/2), where the highest value of the sum was 9, and therefore the highest value of SPEC_PROJ was 5. SPEC_ATTND was just the sum of SPEC1A + SPEC2A + SPEC3A, each of which was the reported "highest attendance" during the last two years for attendance at each type of event.

In all Birmingham neighborhoods, NEWSFREQ was assumed to be 20 (they are mailed out to all households in all neighborhoods by the CRO's from city hall), and NEWSDIST was assumed to be all households (33.3 percent of population).

Dayton	*Value Range*	*Variable Name*
12. Has organization recently been reconstituted?	y or n	REORG
(This variable was only used to evaluate default values where information was not otherwise available. A reorganized group was assumed to have been in existence only during one third of the two-year period in question)		
13. Does organization regularly send representatives to higher body?	0 to 3	REP
0 = no NA representative, no precinct represenative		
1 = no NA representative, some precinct representatives		
2 = 1 NA representative and up to 4 precinct representatives, or no NA representative but 5 or more precinct representatives		
3 = 2 NA representatives, or 1 NA representative and 5 or more precinct representatives		
14. Number of organizers active in all events during the last two years (sum)	0 to 200	SPEC_ORGZ

Virtually all neighborhoods with any organization at all had neighborhood needs prepared (if necessary by Priority Board Staff), so this was not used in the analysis.

The default value used in Dayton for number of newsletters was 6, the default number of households receiving newsletter was one-half (or one-sixth of population).

The SPEC_PROJ item was evaluated directly from the raw neighborhood reports, with the rating representing approximately the number of valid projects described. When five or more valid projects were described a rating of 5 was assigned. SPEC_ATTND represents the sum of attendance at all valid events listed.

The Dayton budget information does not include the Priority Board budgets.

Portland	Value Range	Variable Name
12. Does organization regularly send representative to higher body? (to at least 80% of district coalition board meetings)	y or n	REP
13. Does organization send in neighborhood needs statements each year?	y or n	NEEDS
14. Coordrate (for some neighborhoods only) This rating made directly by the district coalition staff member interviewed. (Not used in analysis at this time.)	0 to 7	COORDRATE

For ELECTIONS, Portland has a value of "0," "1," or "2" per 2 years.

The Portland budget information does not include funds used by the District Coalition for the support of neighborhood newsletters, training, etc.

SPEC_PROJ was assessed directly from the raw data, roughly proportional to the number and relationship of events to organizational objectives. The rating goes from 0 to 4. In some neighborhoods, very little information was available to provide an accurate rating, but an estimate was made wherever possible. SPEC_ATTND represents the sum of all the attendance figures noted for the special events.

St. Paul	Value Range	Variable Name
12. Does organization regularly send representatives to higher body? (All are y; not used in analysis.)	y or n	REP
13. Attendance at annual meeting (average last two years)	# people	ANNUAL_MTG
14. Degree of block club organization	0 to 5	BLOCKCLUBS

1 = 1 to 5 block clubs active
2 = 6 to 30 block clubs active
3 = 31 to 100 block clubs active
4 = 101 to 200 block clubs active
5 = more than 200 block clubs active

15. Does organization undertake special organizational outreach efforts? 1 = Council does extensive sign posting, flyering in addition to the newspaper, and/or major phone outreach	0 or 1	SPEC_OUT
16. Number of staff members of Council	# FET people	STAFF
17. Amount of budget raised exclusive of city allocation	$ amount	BUDRAISE

Several St. Paul items were constant: all ELECTIONS were "y," all OFFICERS were "y," and all REG_MEET were 24. REG_ATTEND was the average attendance at a regular Council meeting. NEWSALL was not used in St. Paul.

SPEC_PROJ was coded from 1 to 4:

    1 = Only general projects like recycling and cleanup
    2 = General projects plus up to 2 committees or specific projects.
    3 = General projects plus up to 5 committees or specific projects.
    4 = General projects plus more than 5 committees or specific projects

SPEC_ATTEND was the sum of all involvement figures given by District Council staff for specific projects mentioned. The overall "number of people involved during the year," when given, occasionally ranged wildly higher than this sum, and was discounted.

All District Councils have their own neighborhood newspaper, or access to one. In most cases the newspaper is distributed to all households in the District, but only a portion of the newspaper deals with the Council activities. Therefore, NEWSDIST was calculated by allocating a specific percentage of coverage for the amount of material included in the newspaper. The following percentages were used:

    One Column = 10%   One Page = 20%
    One Article = 10%   Front Page = 5%

The totals of these percentages, up to 100%, were used for NEWSDIST. In some cases an average coverage between two district newspapers was needed (adding the frequencies).

BUDGET figures in St. Paul include all money expended by the District Council, including the amount received from the city.

Appendix D

Construction of the Index of Neighborhood Organizational Strength

The index was created from the three separate measures of core strength, outreach, and involvement described in Appendix C. Our operating assumption is that a strong neighborhood organization needs to demonstrate high capacity in each of these areas. A simple additive scale therefore would be inappropriate. Instead, we adopted a model that provides the highest strength ratings for neighborhoods with high results on each of the three separate measures, and lowers that rating in proportion to a reduction on any of the measures. The outreach and involvement ratings were given slight priority in the sense that a strong showing on each can overcome some weakness in the core strength measure.

The definitions of each level of the index as based on the three separate measures expressed as a triplet (L,M,H) where VL = Very Low, L = Low, M = Moderate, H = High, and VH = Very High on the respective measure of core strength, outreach, or involvement.

Basic Rule	Fine Tuning
Level 1. All three are low or very low i.e. (L,L,VL)	Also includes (M,VL,VL) *St. Paul: both low or very low (L,VL)
Level 2: Any two are low or very low i.e. (M,L,L)	Also includes (M,M,VL) *St. Paul: only one low or very low (M,L)
Level 3: Only one is low or very low i.e. (H,M,L)	*St. Paul: no low or very low (H,M)
Level 4: None are low, or very low, but all are not high or very high i.e. (H,M,M)	Also includes (L,H,M) where the low value is only in the core *St. Paul: both high, but not both very high (H,H)
Level 5: All are high or very high i.e. (VH,VH,H)	Also includes (M,H,H) where the moderate value is only in core *St. Paul: both very high (VH,VH)

* In St. Paul, the core strength measures available were not useful in distinguishing between neighborhood groups, so only the outreach and involvement measures were used, as indicated in the fine-tuning column.

To determine what was a very high, high, moderate, low, or very low value, a series of cut points were used on each of the three measures. The cut points varied from city to city because a wide range of different factors entered into the calculation of the scale in each case, as we noted in Appendix C. The cut points are necessarily somewhat subjective, but were chosen for each city after consideration of all the elements involved in each scale and their usefulness in distinguishing between neighborhoods in that city. In the table below, each value represents the highest scores on the scale that were included in that category.

Cut Points on Each Component Scale

	Birmingham			Dayton			Portland			St. Paul		
	Core	Out.	Invol.	Core	Out.	Invol.	Core	Out.	Invol.	Core	Out.	Invol.
Very Low (VL)	0	1.5	1.4	0	0.5	0.5	0	1.0	0.8	*	1.0	0.5
Low (L)	1	3.0	2.5	1	1.0	2.0	1	1.5	1.1	*	2.0	1.5
Moderate (M)	3	3.5	3.5	2	3.0	3.5	3	2.0	1.5	*	2.5	2.0
High (H)	4	4.5	4.5	3	4.0	5.0	4	3.0	2.0	*	4.8	3.0
Very High (H)	>4	>4.5	>4.5	>3	>4.0	>5.0	>4	>3.0	>2.0	*	>4.8	>3.0

For example:

A neighborhood in Birmingham had values of 3.0, 2.8, and 1.9 on the three scales in that city. It was rated (M,L,L), and thus was assigned a neighborhood organization strength level of 2.

A neighborhood in Dayton had values of 3.0, 5.5 and 2.4, giving it a rating of (M,VH,M) and a consequent strength level of 4.

A neighborhood in Portland had values of 5.0, 2.8 and 2.1, giving it a rating of (VH,H,VH) with resulting strength level of 5.

A neighborhood in St. Paul had values of 4.7 and 1.8 on the outreach and involvement scales, giving it a rating of (H,M) with resulting strength level of 3.

Appendix E

Construction of the Index of Neighborhood Socioeconomic Status

The Index of Neighborhood Socioeconomic Status was developed by grouping together neighborhoods which had similar values across a range of six income and education items from the federal Neighborhood Statistics Program. Each is an aggregate statistic for an individual neighborhood:

I = Median household income
A = Percent of households with public assistance income
U = Percent of civilian labor force unemployed
P = Percent of persons below the poverty level
C = Percent of persons age 25 or over having attended at least 4 years college
H = Percent of persons age 25 or over having graduated from high school

For each statistic, the mean and standard deviation was calculated across all the cities of our study (including defined neighborhoods covering about half the city of San Antonio, the fifth city in our larger study, which was not part of the analysis in this book). In the case of income, the ratio of median household income in the neighborhood to median household income of the city was calculated first, and the remaining operations performed on that ratio. This was done under the assumption that the appropriate variable is a measure of relative income within a community, rather than of absolute dollar income. The resulting values are indicated in the table on the top of page 172.

Once these values were calculated, the census data for each neighborhood was expressed in terms of standard deviations from the mean, rounded to the nearest integer. A value of $X = -2$, therefore, implies that the unemployment rate in that neighborhood was between -1.50 and -2.49 standard deviations from the mean unemployment rate for all neighborhoods in our sample. The neighborhoods were then grouped on the basis of these values, treating the economic variables (income, assistance, poverty, and unemployment) and the education variables (college and high school) as two independent measures. Within the

	Value Across All Cities in Sample			
Variable	Mean	Std. Dev.	Maximum	Minimum
Income Ratio	1.02	0.43	2.74	0.25
Assistance (%)	12.13	9.69	55.26	0.00
Unemployment (%)	9.30	6.45	47.90	0.00
Poverty (%)	20.07	14.29	80.80	0.00
College (%)	13.24	13.34	67.82	0.00
High School (%)	59.97	19.97	98.40	10.50

Note: The 1980 citywide median household income values used to calculate the income ratios were: Birmingham, $12,157; Dayton, $12,068; Portland, $14,804; St. Paul, $16,029. On a neighborhood basis across all cities, median household income averaged $13,577 with a maximum of $38,328 and a minimum of $3,750.

economic variables, the income ratio had the greatest weight in determining the grouping, with the other three variables being of lesser weight, generally having an impact on the grouping only if all three deviated in the same direction from the typical values of the income-based group. Within the education variables, high school graduation was the dominant figure determining the ordering, with college education having lesser weight.

The resulting groupings, and the values that determine them, are listed below. The rightmost column lists the number of neighborhoods in the four-city sample with the characteristics indicated on that row.

	Income Measures				Education		
	I	A	U	P	H	C	Exceptions[c]
1. Very low income							
VL1	-2	$-1,-3$ or -4	$0,-4,$ or -6	$-2,-3,$ or -4	$-1,-2$	-1	
VL2	-1	$-1,-2$[b]	$-1,-2$[b]	$-1,-2$[b]	$-1,-2$	-1	D14, B45: H = 0
							D15: C = 0
VL3	-1	-2	-2	-2	$-1,-2$	-1	D32: C = 0
2. Low income, low education							
LL1	-1	$-1,-2$[a]	$-1,-2$[a]	$-1,-2$[a]	$-1,-2$	-1	B68:U = 0; D25: A = 0
LL2	-1	-1	-1	-1	$-1,-2$	-1	
LL3	-1	$0,-1$[a]	$0,-1$[a]	$0,-1$[a]	$-1,-2$	-1	D60: C = 0
LL4	0	-1	$-1,-2$	-1	$-1,-2$	-1	D62, D64: P = 0, U = -2
3. Low income, moderate education							
LM1	-1	$-1,-2$[a]	$-1,-2$[a]	$-1,-2$[a]	0	$0,-1$	B34: U = 0, P = -2
							P45: P = 0, A = -1
LM2	-1	$0,-1$[a]	$0,-1$[a]	$0,-1$[a]	0	$0,-1$	P26: A = U = P = -1
LM3	0	-1	-1	-1	0	$0,-1$	

Moderate income, low education

−1	0	0	0	−1,−2	−1		1
−1	0	1	0	−1,−2	−1		0
0	0,−1[a]	0,−1[a]	0,−1[a]	−1,−2	−1	B42: C = 0, P = 1	7
0	0	0	0	−1,−2	−1		3
0	0,1[a]	0,1[a]	0,1[a]	−1,−2	−1	P16: C = 0	1

Moderate income, moderate education

#							
1	−1	0	0	0	0,1	0,−1	B71: U = 1, P = −1 — 5
2	−1	0,1[a]	0,1[a]	0,1[a]	0,1	0,−1	3
3	0	0,−1[a]	0,−1[a]	0,−1[a]	0,1	0,−1	12
4	0	0	0	0	0,1	0	P49: U = −1, A = 1 — 18
							B25: U=1, A=−1
5	0	0,1[a]	0,1[a]	0,1[a]	0,1	0,−1	29
6	1	0,−1[a]	0,−1[a]	0,−1[a]	0,1	0,−1	D3: U = −1, P = 1 — 3

Moderate income, high education

#							
1	−1	0	0	0	1	1	3
2	0	0	0	0	1	1	P75: I = −1, U = A = P=1 — 4
							D70: A = 1, P = −2
3	0	0,1[a]	0,1[a]	0,1[a]	1	1	2

Moderate income, very high education

#							
1	−1	0,1	0	1	1	2,3	P31: E = −1 — 2
2	0	1	1	0,1	1,2	2,3	4

High income, moderate education

#							
1	0	1	1	1	0,1	0,−1	8
2	1	0,1[a]	0,1[a]	0,1[a]	0,1	0,−1	B86: A = U = P = 0 — 12
							D38, D 72: U = −1
3	1	1	1	1	0,1	0	9
4	2	1	1	1	1	0	B9: A = 0 — 9
							B24: H = 2; B39: C = −1

High income, high education

0	1	1	1	1	1		6
1	1	1	1	1	1	D21: U = −1; B36: P = 0	5
1	1	1	1	1,2	2	P28: U = 0	12
2	1	1	1	1	1	D33: U = 0	4
2	1	1	1	1,2	2		4

Very high income

3	1	1	1	1,2	1	D29: U = 0; B75: C = 0	3
3,4	1	1	1	2	3,4		5

s:

ll values in the second through sixth columns of the table represent the number of standard deviations from
ne mean of all neighborhoods in the sample.

a. All three values of A, U, P not being the same.
b. And at least one of these values is −3 or −4.
c. These exceptions are deviations from the rule represented in that row. Each exception is given in the form: City Neighborhood-Number: Variable = Value. For example, D33: U = 0 means that Dayton neighborhood number 33 has unemployment equal to 0 standard deviations from the mean of unemployment for all neighborhoods in the sample.

Appendix F

Regression Equation for the Participation Difference (PD) Calculation

In order to understand the impact of neighborhood and neighborhood organizational strength upon participation levels and consequences, we developed an equation which could predict the likelihood that an individual would be a participant in the neighborhood system based on individual demographic characteristics alone.

The earlier work of our research team found that education, income, age, race, home ownership, and length of residence were all highly correlated with political participation. We therefore extracted the information from the public opinion surveys that dealt with each of these characteristics, and recoded each into an approximately linear form against participation levels. For example, participation increases with age up to age 45 and then begins to decrease as age continues to increase. A new variable was created, which might be called the age predictor of participation, which coded the age categories up to age 45 in a linear fashion, and then coded the age categories from 45–95 in a descending linear fashion. These two recodings were then combined into a single scale, against which participation is approximately linear. A regression equation was chosen because of its robust ability to predict the value of the dependent variable, in this case participation, under the assumption of linear and additive relationships to the independent "demographic predictor" variables created as we just described.

The variables used in this equation were:

Dependent Variable:
> PARTIC (whether respondent has participated in NA in last two years; value range 0 to 1)

Independent Variables:
> INC (annual household income: value range 1 to 6 representing incomes from below $5000 to above $75,000)
>
> ED (education level of respondent: value range 1 to 7 representing education level from "some high school" to "advanced degree")

AGE (age of respondent; value ranges 1 to 6 representing ages from 18 to 95)
RACE (race category of respondent: value range 1 to 3 representing white, black,
   Hispanic and "other" racial and ethnic categories)
HOME (home ownership status of respondents and spouse; value range 1 to 3
   representing "ownership," "renting," and "other" categories)
RESID (length of residence at this address; value range 1 to 4 representing num-
   ber of years from less than one to more than eleven)

The final stepwise regression (with pairwise deletion of missing values) re-
tained all variables, yielding:

Multiple R .31320
R Square .09810
Analysis of Variance: F = 73.9, Signif at .0000
Standardized Beta Coefficients:

		T value	Signif. of T
ED	.179560	10.987	.0000
AGE	.116072	7.198	.0000
RACE	.102293	6.854	.0000
HOME	.058734	3.189	.0014
RESID	.073281	4.109	.0000
INC	.060714	3.548	.0004

and a resulting equation predicting the likelihood that an individual will be a
participant:

$$\text{PPRED} = -.3767 + .0389 \times \text{EDUC} + .0314 \times \text{AGE} + .0720 \times \text{RACE} +$$
$$.0232 \times \text{HOME} + .0207 \times \text{RESID} + .0177 \times \text{INC}$$

where PPRED ranges from 0 (0% likelihood of participation) to 1 (100%
likelihood of participation)

and the coefficients for each independent variable are just the unstandardized
regression coefficients from the regression calculation. It is worth noting what
this equation means for the maximum impact of each variable upon the predicted participation levels. For example, all other things being equal, the predicted difference in the rate of participation between a neighborhood in which
all residents have the highest education levels and one in which all residents
have the lowest education levels is 23 percent of the total population. The corresponding values for the other variables are listed below:

max. impact of:	
education	23%
age	16%
race	14%
home ownership	5%
length of residency	6%
income	9%

Finally, we can calculate the difference between the prediction for participation and the actual value for participation, as:

$$\text{PD} = 100 \times (\text{PPRED} - \text{PARTIC}) \quad (\text{value range } -100\% \text{ to } +100\%)$$

where for any group of individuals (e.g., survey respondents from one neighborhood), the mean value of PD is just the difference between the percentage of the group who are predicted to be participants (the mean value of PPRED for this group), and the actual percentage of the group who are participants (mean value of PARTIC for this group).

Notes

1. Representative vs. Participatory Government (pp. 1–7)

1. Stephen C. Craig, *The Malevolent Leaders* (San Francisco: Westview Press, 1993).
2. The degree to which this assumed stability of democratic forms in unrealistic can be seen in James A. Morone's examination of the epic struggles between the yearning for democracy and the dread of big government in American history, in *The Democratic Wish: Popular Participation and the Limits of American Government* (New Haven, Conn.: Yale University Press, 1998; originally published in 1990 by Basic Books).
3. Robert N. Bellah, Richard Madsen, William M. Sullivan, Ann Swidler, and Steven M. Tipton, *Habits of the Heart: Individualism and Commitment in American Life* (New York: Harper and Row, 1985); followed by *The Good Society* (New York: Knopf, 1991).
4. Robert Putnam, *Making Democracy Work: Civic Traditions in Modern Italy* (Princeton: Princeton University Press, 1993).
5. Robert Putnam, "Bowling Alone: America's Declining Social Capital," *Journal of Democracy* 6 (January 1995), pp. 65–78. He brings substantially more data to bear on these same issues in his subsequent book, *Bowling Alone: The Collapse and Revival of American Community* (New York: Simon and Schuster, 2000).
6. See, for example, the excellent review by Jean Cohen in "Trust, Voluntary Association and Workable Democracy: The Contemporary American Discourse of Civil Society," *Democracy and Trust,* ed. Mark E. Warren (Cambridge: Cambridge University Press, 1999), pp. 208–48; also see Margaret Levi, "Social and Unsocial Capital: A Review Essay of Robert Putnam's *Making Democracy Work,*" *Politics and Society* 24 (March 1996), pp. 45–55; and Alejandro Portes and Patricia Landolt, "The Downside of Social Capital," *The American Prospect* 26 (May/June 1996), pp. 18–21, 94.
7. Important findings in the opposite direction include those presented by Sidney Verba, Kay Schlozman, Kay Lehman, and Henry E. Brady, *Voice and Equality: Voluntarism in American Politics* (Cambridge, Mass.: Harvard University Press, 1995); and by the Pew Research Center for the People and the Press, *Trust and Citizen Engagement in Metropolitan Philadelphia: A Case Study* (Washington, D.C.: The Pew Research Center, 1997).
8. Cohen, "Trust, Voluntary Association and Workable Democracy," p. 216.
9. See, for example, David B. Truman, *The Governmental Process* (New York: Knopf, 1951), pp. 139–55.
10. The data for this book represents a portion of that collected as part of a larger study on the impact of citizen participation on policy responsiveness, local governance, and citizen capacity-building. The results of the larger study are reported in Jeffrey M. Berry, Kent E. Portney, and Ken Thomson, *The Rebirth of Urban Democracy* (Washington, D.C.: Brookings Institution, 1993).
11. For an overview, see Albert Hunter, "The Loss of Community: An Empirical Test Through Replication," *American Sociological Review* 40 (1975), pp. 537–52.

12. Jack L. Walker, "The Origins and Maintenance of Interest Groups in America," *American Political Science Review* 77 (June 1983), pp. 390–406.

2. The Aggregation of Interests (pp. 8–32)

1. J. Roland Pennock, *Democratic Political Theory* (Princeton, N.J.: Princeton University Press, 1979), pp. 309–10.
2. Hanna Fenichel Pitkin, *The Concept of Representation* (Berkeley and Los Angeles: University of California Press, 1967).
3. Pitkin, *Concept of Representation,* p. 121, elaborated on pp. 127–39. She also examines a fourth classification, that of "deputy," as well as a number of significant shadings of each of these areas, but concludes (p. 139) that three major concepts underlie all of these uses of representation in the sense of "acting for." These three concepts I have embodied here in the terms "trustee," "delegate," and "agent."
4. Thomas Hobbes, "Of Persons, Authors and Things Personated," chapter 16, *Leviathan* (Indianapolis: Bobbs-Merrill, 1977; originally published in 1651), pp. 132–36.
5. A. Phillips Griffiths and Richard Wollheim, "How Can One Person Represent Another?" *Aristotelian Society,* Suppl. 34 (1960), pp. 187–224.
6. Pennock, *Democratic Political Theory,* p. 314.
7. Griffiths and Wollheim, "One Person," p. 190. Pitkin's comment (p. 269) in reference to this work is worth repeating: "Anyone who questions whether the insane man, the favorite example of political philosophers, has relevance to the realities of political life is referred to this item from the *San Francisco Chronicle,* November 10, 1960: 'Aroma (France), Nov. 9 (UPI)—Mayor Pierre Echalon complained today that it is impossible to run this French village sensibly because mental cases outnumber sane citizens in the local electorate. Echalon told provincial authorities that population of Aroma consists of 148 normal villagers and 161 patients in a mental hospital, who through a quirk in the law enjoy full voting privileges. Provincial officials promised to 'look into the matter.'"
8. Pitkin, *Concept of Representation,* p. 209.
9. Pennock, *Democratic Political Theory,* pp. 321 ff.
10. Lani Guinier, *The Tyranny of the Majority: Fundamental Fairness in Representative Democracy* (New York: The Free Press, 1994), esp. pp. 149 ff.
11. Jane J. Mansbridge, *Beyond Adversary Democracy* (Chicago: University of Chicago Press, 1983; original copyright 1980), pp. 31–33. She sums up her central critique of consensus processes thus: "Groups that are accustomed to using consensus find it hard to recognize and to legitimate conflicts of interest by allowing bargains, distributing benefits proportionately, taking turns, or making decisions by majority rule. Just like couples who feel they must act on every issue as if they were one, consensual groups often find themselves unable to shift to adversary techniques when their members' interests begin to conflict. Such groups end up either reinforcing the status quo or, in an informal and unacknowledged manner, forcing the minority to go along."
12. Robert A. Dahl, *A Preface to Democratic Theory* (Chicago: University of Chicago Press, 1956), p. 128.

13. Jeffrey M. Berry, Kent E. Portney, and Ken Thomson, *The Rebirth of Urban Democracy,* pp. 53–54. Entries on the left hand side of this table are adopted from Dahl, *Preface,* p. 84.
14. In John S. Saloma III and Frederick H. Sontag, *Parties: The Real Opportunity for Effective Citizen Politics* (New York: Alfred A. Knopf, 1972), p. xi.
15. Norman H. Nie, "Citizen Participation in a Declining Party System: Participating More and Enjoying It Less," in *Citizen Participation Perspectives,* ed. Stuart Langton (Medford, Mass.: Lincoln Filene Center, 1979), p. 168.
16. Everett Carll Ladd, *Where Have All The Voters Gone?* (New York: Norton, 1982), pp. xx–xxi.
17. Walter Dean Burnham, "The Onward March of Party Decomposition," in *Controversies in American Voting Behavior,* ed. Richard G. Niemi and Herbert F. Weisberg (San Francisco: W. H. Freeman, 1976), p. 431.
18. Austin Ranney, *The Doctrine of Responsible Party Government* (Urbana: University of Illinois Press, 1954), p. 12.
19. Everett Carll Ladd, Jr., *American Political Parties* (New York: W. W. Norton, 1970), pp. 8–9.
20. Nie, "Citizen Participation," pp. 166–67.
21. Clinton Rossiter, *Parties and Politics in America* (Ithaca, N.Y.: Cornell University Press, 1960), p. 11.
22. Anthony Downs, *An Economic Theory of Democracy* (New York: Harper Bros., 1957), chap. 8.
23. See for example, Paul F. Lazarsfeld, Bernard Berelson, and Hazel Gaudet, *The People's Choice* (New York: Columbia University Press, 1944), p. 142; Bernard R. Berelson, Paul F. Lazarsfeld, and William N. McPhee, *Voting* (Chicago: University of Chicago Press, 1954), p. 89, and Norman H. Nie, Sidney Verba, and John R. Petrocik, *The Changing American Voter* (Cambridge, Mass.: Harvard University Press, 1979), pp. 51 and 363–64.
24. See especially Austin Ranney, *Doctrine,* pp. 125–51.
25. Austin Ranney and Willmoore Kendall, *Democracy and the American Party System* (Westport, Conn.: Greenwood Press, 1974), p. 499.
26. See David Butler, "American Myths about British Parties," *Virginia Quarterly Review* 21 (Winter 1955), pp. 46–56; Pendleton Herring, *The Politics of Democracy* (New York: Rinehart, 1940), pp. 53–59; Donald K. Price, "The Parliamentary and Presidential Systems," *Public Administration Review,* 3 (Autumn 1943), pp. 317–34; and Arthur N. Holcombe, *Our More Perfect Union* (Cambridge, Mass.: Harvard University Press, 1950), pp. 410–11.
27. E. E. Schattschneider, *Party Government* (New York: Rinehart, 1942), pp. 58–59.
28. Roberto Michels, *Political Parties* (New York: Dover, 1915), pp. 32–33.
29. Max Weber, *From Max Weber: Essays in Sociology* (New York: Oxford University Press, 1958), p. 253.
30. Mayer Zald and Roberta Ash, "Social Movement Organizations: Growth, Decay, and Change," *Social Forces* 44 (March 1966), p. 327.
31. Jo Freeman, *The Politics of Women's Liberation* (New York: David McKay, 1975), pp. 49–70.

32. Ralph H. Turner and Lewis Killian, *Collective Behavior* (Englewood Cliffs, N.J.: Prentice-Hall, 1957), p. 84.
33. Neil L. Smelser, *Theory of Collective Behavior* (New York: Free Press, 1962).
34. See, for example, Gary T. Marx and James L. Wood in *Annual Review of Sociology* (Palo Alto, Calif.: Annual Reviews, 1975), ed. Alex Inkeles, pp. 406–13, for a review of attempts to test Smelser's theories.
35. Arthur Bentley, *The Process of Government* (Cambridge, Mass.: Harvard University Press, 1967; originally published 1908), pp. 222, 211.
36. David Truman, *Governmental Process* (New York: Alfred A. Knopf, 1951), pp. 35, 51.
37. James Q. Wilson, *Political Organizations* (New York: Basic Books, 1973), pp. 3–7.
38. Anthony Oberschall, *Social Conflict and Social Movements* (Englewood Cliffs, N.J.: Prentice-Hall, 1973), p. 28.
39. Zald and Ash, "Social Movement Organizations," esp. p. 334.
40. Edward Walsh, in *Research in Social Movements, Conflicts, and Change* (Greenwich, Conn.: JAI Press, 1978), p. 155.
41. Robert Dahl, *Preface, p.* 137.
42. E. E. Schattschneider, *The Semisovereign People* (Hinsdale, Ill.: The Dryden Press, 1975; original edition, 1960), pp. 34–35.
43. Heather Booth, "New Directions for the Citizen Movement," *Citizen Action News* 2:1 (Winter 1981), p. 1.
44. Theodore J. Lowi, *The End of Liberalism* (New York: Norton, 1979), pp. 62–63.
45. E. E. Schattschneider, *Party Government* (New York: Rinehart, 1942), p. 52.
46. John D. McCarthy and Mayer N. Zald, "Resource Mobilization and Social Movements: A Partial Theory," *American Journal of Sociology* 82:6 (1977), pp. 1231–32.
47. Charles Tilly, *From Mobilization to Revolution* (Reading, Mass.: Addison-Wesley, 1978), pp. 151–58.
48. Saul Alinsky began a tradition in the 1940s of populist, confrontational, throughly unconventional community organizing that hundreds of organizations have since emulated. We will be exploring the activities of these organizations in much more detail in Chapter 5.
49. Heather Booth, "New Directions," p. 2.
50. Zald and Ash, "Social Movement Organizations," pp. 333–34.

3. Participatory Alternatives (pp. 33–49)

1. Juliet Saltman, "Neighborhood Change: Facts, Perceptions, Prospects," *Housing and Society* 13 (1986), pp. 136–59.
2. Thomas Wilson, "White Response to Neighborhood Racial Change," *Sociological Focus* 16 (1983), pp. 305–18.
3. Harvey Molotock, *Managed Integration* (Berkeley: University of California Press, 1972).
4. Gerald D. Suttles, *The Social Order of the Slum* (Chicago: University of Chicago Press, 1968); followed by his work, *The Social Construction of Communities* (Chicago: University of Chicago Press, 1972).

5. Albert Hunter, *Symbolic Communities* (Chicago: University of Chicago Press, 1974).

6. Gary Orfield, *Neighborhood Change and Integration in Metropolitan Chicago* (Report to Metropolitan Leadership Council, Chicago: University of Chicago, 1984).

7. Richard P. Taub, *Paths of Neighborhood Change: Race and Crime in Urban America* (Chicago: University of Chicago Press, 1984).

8. Juliet Saltman, *A Fragile Movement: The Struggle for Neighborhood Stabilization* (New York: Greenwood Press, 1990).

9. Anthony Downs, *Neighborhoods and Urban Development* (Washington, D.C.: Brookings Institution, 1981).

10. Arthur J. Naparstek and Gale Cincotta, *Urban Disinvestment: New Implications for Community Organization, Research, and Public Policy* (Washington, D.C.: National Center for Urban Ethnic Affairs, 1976).

11. Rick Cohen, "Neighborhoods, Planning, and Political Capacity," *Urban Affairs Quarterly* 14:3 (March 1979), pp. 337–62.

12. Louis Wirth, "Urbanism as a Way of Life," *American Journal of Sociology* 44 (July 1938), pp. 1–24.

13. Robert A. Nisbet, *The Quest for Community* (New York: Oxford University Press, 1953).

14. Maurice Stein, *The Eclipse of Community* (New York: Harper and Row, 1960).

15. J. D. Kasarda and M. Janowitz, "Community Attachment in Mass Society," *American Sociological Review* 39:3 (June 1974), pp. 328–39.

16. Jane Jacobs, *The Death and Life of Great American Cities* (New York: Random House, 1961).

17. Herbert Gans, *The Urban Villagers* (New York: Free Press, 1962).

18. C. S. Fischer, *To Dwell Among Friends: Personal Networks in Town and City* (Chicago: University of Chicago Press, 1982).

19. For the survey process used to select these cities, see the methodological appendix of Jeffrey M. Berry, Kent E. Portney, and Ken Thomson, *The Rebirth of Urban Democracy* (Washington, D.C.: Brookings Institution, 1993), pp. 301–3. The fifth city that was part of this study, San Antonio, does not have a citywide neighborhood system, and therefore was not included for study in this book. Appendix A provides an overview of the basic demographics of each city.

20. Berry, Portney, and Thomson, *Rebirth*. An explanation of the sampling framework and development of the overall public opinion questionnaires and interview instruments is provided on pp. 304–15.

21. See, for example, Scott Greer, "Urbanism Reconsidered: A Comparative Study of Local Areas in a Metropolis," *American Sociological Review* 21 (1956), pp. 19–25; as well as Suttles, *Social Order* (1982) and Hunter, *Symbolic Communities* (1974).

22. See Robert L. Lineberry, *Equality and Urban Policy: The Distribution of Municipal Public Services* (Beverly Hills, Calif.: Sage, 1977); and D. Harvey, *Social Justice and the City* (Baltimore: Johns Hopkins University Press, 1973).

23. See, for example, Joseph F. Zimmerman, "Neighborhoods and Citizen Involvement," *Public Administration Review* 32 (May/June 1972), pp. 201–10; Howard

W. Hallman, *Neighborhoods: Their Place In Urban Life* (Beverly Hills: Sage Publications, 1984); and H. J Schmandt, "Decentralization: A Structural Imperative," *Neighborhood Control in the 1970s: Politics, Administration and Citizen Participation* (New York: Chandler Publishing, 1973).

24. W. Bell and M. D. Boat, "Urban Neighborhoods and Informal Social Relations," *American Journal of Sociology* 62 (1957), pp. 391–98; and J. D. Kasarda and M. Janowitz, "Community Attachment in Mass Society," *American Sociological Review* 39:3 (June 1974), pp. 328–39.
25. See Jeffrey Pressman and Aaron Wildavsky, *Implementation* (Berkeley: University of California, 1973).
26. Abraham Wandersman, "A Framework of Participation in Community Organizations," *The Journal of Applied Behavioral Science* 17 (1981), pp. 27–58.
27. Douglas Yates, *Neighborhood Democracy: The Politics and Impacts of Decentralization* (Lexington, Mass.: D. C. Heath, 1973); his rating scale is summarized on p. 82.
28. Berry, Portney, and Thomson, *Rebirth;* see especially the table on page 84.

4. The Participatory Core (pp. 50–72)

1. See Jeffrey M. Berry, Kent E. Portney, and Ken Thomson, *The Rebirth of Urban Democracy* (Washington, D.C.: Brookings Institution, 1993), pp. 301–3, for a discussion of the methodology of the larger survey of our research team, which collected information on 900 participation efforts and ended up with 70 models of strong participation.
2. G. D. H. Cole, *Guild Socialism* (New York: Stokes, 1920), p. 24.
3. See Appendix B of this book, St. Paul Section C1, for a more complete description of the Capital Improvement Budget Committee (CIB).
4. Peter Bachrach and Morton S. Baratz, "Two Faces of Power," *American Political Science Review* 56 (December 1962), pp. 947–52.
5. Norman H. Nie, Sidney Verba, and John R. Petrocik, *The Changing American Voter* (Cambridge, Mass.: Harvard University Press, 1979), pp. 123–44.
6. Leonard P. Oliver, *The Art of Citizenship: Public Issue Forums* (Dayton: Kettering Foundation, 1983). The Foundation also has produced issue books designed for citizen discussion on more than twenty topics.
7. One of the best discussions of the appropriate nature of deliberation in a democracy is provided by Benjamin Barber in *Strong Democracy* (Berkeley: University of California Press, 1984). See especially pp. 178–98 for his elaboration of the "Nine Functions of Strong Democratic Talk." An important theoretical framework is provided in John Elser, ed. *Deliberative Democracy* (Cambridge: Cambridge University Press, 1998).
8. On the issues of administrator perception of problems such as delay, conflict, and so on, because of the city's participation system, see Berry, Portney, and Thomson, *Rebirth,* pp. 206–13; on the question of parochialism, see pp. 180–88.
9. Portland City Ordinance No. 159923, of July 19, 1987, p. 1.

5. Aggressive Outreach (pp. 73–92)

1. To capture the gestalt of this approach, see Saul Alinsky, *Rules for Radicals: A Practical Primer for Realistic Radicals* (New York: Random House, 1971).
2. Two good overviews of the Alinsky movement and its implications are provided in Joan Lancourt, *Confront or Concede: The Alinsky Citizen-Action Organizations* (Lexington, Mass.: Lexington Books, 1979); and Sanford D. Horwitt, *Let Them Call Me Rebel: Saul Alinsky, His Life and Legacy* (New York: Alfred A. Knopf, 1989).
3. Gary Delgado, *Organizing the Movement: The Roots and Growth of ACORN* (Philadelphia: Temple University Press, 1986), pp. 63–90.
4. Delgado, *Organizing the Movement,* p. 67.
5. P. Skerry, "Neighborhood COPS," *The New Republic* (February 6, 1984), pp. 21–23, 190.
6. Jeffrey M. Berry, Kent E. Portney, and Ken Thomson, *The Rebirth of Urban Democracy* (Washington, D.C.: Brookings Institution, 1993); see especially the table on p. 84.
7. Ken Thomson, Jeffrey M. Berry, and Kent E. Portney, *Kernels of Democracy* (Medford: Lincoln Filene Center, 1994), p. 16.
8. Berry, Portney, and Thomson, *Rebirth,* pp. 81–89.
9. Based on the 1980 U.S. Census Neighborhood Statistics program for which San Antonio neighborhood development staff specified boundaries for all of the COPS parishes, as well as the few other neighborhoods in the city that had organizations. In our interviews with COPS members and other neighborhood leaders, we were able to verify the substantial accuracy of these boundaries.
10. The participation levels in this table (4.4) result from a pair of questions. We first asked respondents, "Have you ever actually been active in any community or citizen groups or neighborhood associations?" For those who answered "yes," we asked, "What kind of groups have you been active in?" The first response to this question was classified into one of the four categories of groups indicated in this table.
11. Berry, Portney, and Thomson, *Rebirth,* 75–77.
12. We are indebted to the work of John E. Prestby, Abraham Wandersman, Paul Florin, Richard Rich, and David Chavis, "Benefits, Costs, Incentive Management, and Participation in Voluntary Organizations: A Means to Understanding and Promoting Empowerment," *American Journal of Community Psychology* 18 (February 1990), pp. 117–50, from which these questions were derived.

6. The Policy Link (93–108)

1. See, for example, P. L. Berger and R. J. Neuhaus, *To Empower People: From State to Civil Society* (Washington, D.C.: American Enterprise Institute, 1996). This restates the original premise published in 1980 and includes a dozen reviews of the implications that became clear during the interval.

2. The League of Women Voters, *The Report of the Findings of the League Self-Study,* Publ. 545 (Washington, D.C.: League of Women Voters of the United States, 1974).
3. See, for example, John S. Saloma III and Frederick H. Sontag, *Parties: The Real Opportunity for Effective Citizen Politics* (New York: Alfred A. Knopf, 1972).
4. Jeffrey M. Berry, Kent E. Portney, and Ken Thomson, *The Rebirth of Urban Democracy* (Washington, D.C.: Brookings Institution, 1993), pp. 214–31.
5. The Kettering Foundation, *Kettering Report* (Dayton, Ohio: Kettering Foundation, 1987).
6. See, for example, The Food and Drug Administration, *Priority Setting Process* (annual); S. Cohen, et al. "Institutional Learning in a Bureaucracy: The Superfund Community Relations Program," *Proceedings of the U.S. EPA Conference on Management of Uncontrolled Hazardous Waste Sites,* October 28–30, 1981 (Hazardous Materials Control Research Institute, Silver Spring, Md.), pp. 405–10; *Public Involvement in the Corps of Engineers Planning Process,* U.S. Army Engineer Institute for Water Resources, October 1975); Lawrence Johnson and Associates, *Citizen Participation in Community Development: A Catalog of Local Approaches* (Washington, D.C.: U.S. Department of Housing and Urban Development, July 1978).
7. Senator Mark Hatfield, *The Neighborhood Government Act of 1975,* S.2192.

7. Further Explorations (pp. 109–114)

1. Michael J. Sandel, *Democracy's Discontent: America in Search of a Public Philosophy* (Cambridge, Mass.: Harvard University Press, 1996), p. 350. The opening quotation of this chapter is from pp. 201–2 in the same work.
2. For an insightful review of our state of understanding about these issues, see Michael X. Delli Carpini and Scott Keeter, *What Americans Know About Politics and Why It Matters* (New Haven, Conn.: Yale University Press, 1996). A recent analysis that directly examines the potential of deliberation itself to increase citizen capacity can be found in Fay Lomax Cook, Jason Barabas, and Lawrence R. Jacobs, "Deliberative Democracy in Action: An Analysis of the Effects of Public Deliberation" (Manuscript, Evanston, Ill.: Institute for Policy Research, Northwestern University, December 10, 1999).

Index